The Professional Programmers Guide to
Modula-2

GW00775683

The Professional Programmers Guide to

Modula-2

Robert J Sutherland
Computing Science Department
University of Glasgow

Pitman

PITMAN PUBLISHING
128 Long Acre, London WC2E 9AN

© Robert J Sutherland 1988
First published in Great Britain 1988

British Library Cataloguing in Publication Data
Sutherland, Rob J
  The professional programmers guide to
  Modula-2.—(Professional programmers
  guides).
  1. Modula-2 (Computer program language)
  I. Title
  005.13′3   QA76.73.M63

ISBN 0 273 02577 5

Printed and bound in Great Britain at
The Bath Press, Avon

Contents

Introduction

Although the main aim of this book is to serve as a practical reference source for practicing Modula-2 programmers, the material has been arranged to provide a logical progression of concepts for those readers who are less familiar with the language. No previous programming experience is assumed, so knowledge of older languages such as Pascal or C, although it can be helpful, is not essential.

A special convention is used to describe the form of language constructs. Syntactic entities are indicated by italics, while language symbols are indicated by Courier typeface. A part enclosed by bold square brackets [ ] is optional, ie. it may be omitted or occur once only. A part enclosed by bold curly brackets { } may be omitted or occur any number of times. Spacing is used only for clarity, and has no other significance. Each syntax description is indicated by the symbol > at the left-hand side. For example, in

> E [*sign*] *digit* { *digit* }

the symbol E is a language symbol, while *sign* and *digit* are syntactic entities. A single *sign* may appear if required. A single *digit* is obligatory, but any number of other digits can follow as required.

In the text, Courier typeface is used for all code fragments (including language symbols, example names, expressions, etc.), while italics are used to introduce terms and to indicate values (eg. results of expressions or value-returning procedures). Cross-references to other sections of text are enclosed by angle brackets <>.

Because an agreed standard for Modula-2 does not yet exist and various different versions have had some currency, it is not possible to give a definitive description of some features of the language; the approach followed here is to take account of current usage as provided by various existing implementations, particularly the variant described in the language manual and report which appears in "Programming in Modula-2", 3rd. edition (corrected), by N. Wirth (published by Springer Verlag, 1985). As far as possible, a description is given where any differences or ambiguities might be encountered. These descriptions are highlighted by being enclosed in square brackets [ ].

About the language

Modula-2 was designed by Niklaus Wirth of ETH Zürich, based on experience gained from its notable predecessors, the languages Pascal and Modula. Pascal was originally developed in 1970 as a language for teaching structured programming, and since then has achieved widespread use in many areas of application, largely due to an effective combination of high-level features and implementation efficiency. Modula was an experimental real-time language used to investigate techniques of modular program construction and concurrent programming.

Modula-2 was created with the intention of combining the advantages of both these predecessors to produce a language useable at all levels from high-level data abstraction down to low-level control of hardware, with features well-adapted to the design and construction of practical software. It is already proving to be a worthwhile programming tool for many areas of application and types of installation, including personal computers and single-user workstations.

For convenience, the language is referred to in the following pages simply as Modula.

R. J. Sutherland
University of Glasgow
1988

1 Fundamentals

1.1 General

This chapter describes the basic elements upon which all other language features largely depend; this particularly includes the various characters and symbols from which program constructs are formed. The last section gives a brief introduction to the basic structure of a Modula program, for those readers who are not familiar with the language.

1.2 Basis character set

A minimal character set is defined for use with Modula code. It consists of distinct lower-case and upper-case letters (ie. a-z, A-Z), the decimal digits (ie. 0-9), the space character, and the following special characters:

+	plus
−	minus
*	asterisk
/	slash
=	equals
()	left/right round bracket
[]	left/right square bracket
<>	left/right angle bracket
{}	left/right curly bracket
^	up arrow
#	hash
.,:;	period/comma/colon/semicolon
|	vertical bar
&	ampersand
~	tilde
'	single quote
"	double quote

Additional characters may be available, but they can appear in Modula code only as part of a character-string literal (ie. between single or double quotes) or as part of a comment. [Some implementations, however, do accept the underline character (ie. _) within an identifier <see below>.]

1.3 Identifiers

Identifiers are language symbols which name the various entities in a program (types, constants, variables, procedures and modules). An identifier consists of a contiguous sequence of any number of letters and digits, **commencing with a letter**. For example, the following are all valid identifiers:

```
Windows    Rasters    clear    p33    Date    date
```

Note that the last two identifiers are not equivalent, since upper-case and lower-case letters are considered to be distinct. The following are **not** valid identifiers:

```
9999        33p         error!        @$*&%
```

[Strictly, identifiers containing underline characters, such as

```
this_is_not_an_identifier
```

are not allowed. Nevertheless, underline characters within identifiers are accepted by some implementations, since they can make a complex name much easier to read while preserving the necessary character contiguity. However, code which makes use of this helpful (but non-standard) feature will have to be changed if it is moved to a less tolerant implementation.]

In some cases, *qualified identifiers* are allowed; these are formed by joining simple identifiers together using period characters. Each component of a qualified identifier must be a valid identifier in its own right, and each (except the rightmost) must be a module name. Using the identifiers given above, qualified identifiers such as the following might be possible:

```
Windows.Rasters
```

```
Windows.Rasters.clear
```

```
Date.date
```

1.4 Reserved words

Some identifiers (known as *reserved words*) are used as universal language symbols, and can therefore not be redefined for other uses. The reserved words are:

AND	ARRAY			
BEGIN	BY			
CASE	CONST			
DEFINITION	DIV	DO		
ELSE	ELSIF	END	EXIT	EXPORT
FOR	FROM			
IF	IMPLEMENTATION	IMPORT	IN	
LOOP				
MOD	MODULE			
NOT				
OF	OR			
POINTER	PROCEDURE			
QUALIFIED				
RECORD	REPEAT	RETURN		
SET				
THEN	TO	TYPE		
UNTIL				
VAR				
WHILE	WITH			

1.5 Predefined identifiers

Some identifiers (known as *predefined identifiers*) possess implicit definitions which are universal except where they have been replaced by new definitions. (Redefining a predefined identifier, however, is not usually a particularly useful thing to do.) The predefined identifiers are:

ABS			
BITSET	BOOLEAN		
CAP	CARDINAL	CHAR	CHR
DEC			
EXCL			
FALSE	FLOAT	FLOATD	
HALT	HIGH		
INC	INCL	INTEGER	
LONGCARD	LONGINT	LONGREAL	
MAX	MIN		
NIL			
ODD	ORD		
PROC			
REAL			
SIZE			
TRUE	TRUNC	TRUNCD	
VAL			

3

[SIZE is only a predefined identifier in implementations where it represents a standard procedure <see **Value-returning procedures**, p.93>; in others it is exported from the module SYSTEM <see **Memory-enquiry procedures**, p.81>.]

[FLOATD, LONGCARD, LONGINT, LONGREAL and TRUNCD are also not always predefined identifiers; only implementations which support extended-precision numerical types provide them <see **Standard types**, p.8, and **Standard Procedures**, p.93>.]

1.6 Use of the space character

Space characters are essential for distinguishing language symbols (identifiers, reserved words, etc.) which otherwise would merge; for example, in the statement

```
bool1 :=  NOT bool2
```

a space is required between NOT and bool2, since otherwise a (syntactically-valid) identifier NOTbool2 would be expected.

Spaces cannot be placed within identifiers to punctuate them; in the above statement, for example, a space placed anywhere inside bool1 or bool2 would cause a syntax error.

In all other circumstances, spaces are optional. **Careful use of spaces and blank lines can significantly increase the readability of virtually any software.**

1.7 Comments

A *comment* is any sequence of characters inside the comment bracket symbols (* and *). Comments are provided principally to allow extra information to be inserted into code, and have no effect on program execution. Comments can be embedded within other comments, ie. they can be *nested*. (A technique sometimes used to temporarily disable a section of code is to enclose it in comment brackets. Because nested comments are permitted, no problems arise even if the section already contains comments).

Some examples of valid comments are:

```
(* comments are used to add information *)

(* any available characters can be used: ?@$%! *)

(* this shows a (* nested *) comment *)
```

4

The rules for the placing of comments are the same as those for the placing of space characters <see the previous section>. A comment can occupy any number of lines.

[Comments can sometimes also be used for setting compiler options <see **Using a Typical Implementation**, p.105>.]

1.8 Basic program structure

In Modula, a program is a particular instance of a more general construct, the module <see **Modules**, p.59>. A program module typically takes the following form:

> MODULE *ident* ;
>   { *importClause* }
>   { *declaration* }
>   BEGIN
>   *statement* { ; *statement* }
>   END *ident* .

The identifier *ident* which follows the MODULE and END symbols defines the program name (note the period at the end).

An *importClause* makes identifiers available to the program that are defined externally in a (named) independent module; such a module usually provides a particular service (eg. file management) which can be used by any program that needs it <see **Global modules**, p.61>.

Each *declaration* defines new identifiers of a given type. This is the means by which the various entities in a module (types, constants, variables, procedures and local modules) are created and named <see **Declarations**, p.32>. In a program module, such identifiers are purely local to the program; in a global module they are available to any other module which imports them <see **Modules**, p.59>.

Import clauses must precede declarations, and both must precede the section delimited by the BEGIN and END symbols. The latter describes the sequence of actions which the program performs, each action being specified by a *statement*. A simple statement typically calculates a value using an *expression*, and assigns the value to a named *variable*. A variable is a value-store; it retains the value assigned to it until such time as the value is replaced by a new one. An expression consists of

5

operations performed on values. For example, the statement

```
circ :=  2.0 * pi * radius
```

evaluates the expression 2.0*pi*radius and assigns the result to the variable circ. In this case, the operations performed are two multiplications. The actual operations available depend on the *type* of value involved <see **Types**, p.8>. In this example the values are decimal numbers, ie. of type REAL.

A value can appear in a number of different forms. It can be a *literal constant*, which gives the value directly (eg. 2.0). It can be a *manifest constant*, which is an identifier used to denote a particular value (eg. pi defined to be the value 3.14159) <see **Constant declarations**, p.33>. It can also be the value stored in a given variable (eg. the value of the variable radius), whatever it happens to be when the statement is executed.

A special kind of expression, known as a *constant expression*, is encountered in Modula. This is an expression whose value can be determined directly from the text, ie. no program execution is necessary to evaluate it. (For example, the expression 2.0*pi is a constant expression if pi is a manifest constant.) In some instances, the language definition restricts an expression to being a constant one.

Successive statements must be separated from each other by semicolons. More than one statement can be placed on the same line, and conversely a single statement can extend over any number of lines. A statement can use identifiers which are defined later in the code, provided the definitions are valid in the region of code containing the statement <see **Scope of definitions**, p.38>.

Complex statements can be formed as needed from combinations of the basic ones provided by the language <see **Statements**, p.40>.

As an example of a typical small program module, Figure 1.1 shows a program which calculates factorials. This has one import clause (which imports various input/output procedures from the global module InOut) and one declaration (which creates two local variables of type CARDINAL). The WHILE..DO statement repeatedly multiplies and decrements until the required factorial is produced. The result is written out by the (imported) procedure WriteCard.

(The indentation used in this example is not obligatory, but it helps to make the program structure clear. It is good practice to adopt a consistent system of indentation and faithfully apply it to **all** code.)

```
MODULE factorial;

(* This calculates the factorial *)
(*        of a given number.      *)


FROM InOut IMPORT
  ReadCard,WriteCard,WriteString,WriteLn;

VAR
  value,result : CARDINAL;


BEGIN (*factorial*)

  WriteString("Enter a value (> 0): ");
  ReadCard(value);

  WriteCard(value,8); WriteString("! is ");

  result:= 1;
  WHILE (value > 1) DO
    result:= result * value;
    value:= value - 1
  END; (*WHILE*)

  WriteCard(result,10); WriteLn

END factorial.
```

Figure 1.1: An example program

2 Types

2.1 General

Every value in Modula belongs to some particular *type*. This makes it possible for the compiler to check that values are always used in ways which are consistent with their properties, thereby enhancing program reliability. Each type consists of a *domain* (the range of values which the type possesses) and *operations* (the means by which values are combined to create new ones). Literal constants may also be available, to allow direct representation of particular values.

The available types fall into two categories. *Standard types* are the fundamental types such as characters and numbers which are used by almost every program. They are available as predefined identifiers <see **Predefined identifiers**, p.3>. *User-defined types* make it possible to create new types from standard types and/or other user-defined types. They can be given names by type declarations or be used directly in type and variable declarations <see **Declarations**, p.32>.

2.2 Standard types

The types described here (BOOLEAN, CARDINAL, CHAR, INTEGER and REAL) are provided by all implementations. Other standard types (such as ADDRESS, BITSET and WORD) may also be available, but they can have different properties on different systems; these types are described later <see **Low-Level Facilities**, p.77>.

2.2.1 Type BOOLEAN

The domain of this type consists of the two values *true* and *false* (logical assertion and denial respectively). The value *true* is considered to be greater than *false*. Corresponding literal constants are available in the form of the predefined identifiers TRUE and FALSE.

The operators available with type BOOLEAN are:

AND : *a* AND *b* -> (*b*   if *a* is *true*, else *false*)
OR : *a* OR *b*   -> (*true*   if *a* is *true*, else *b*)
NOT :   NOT *a*   -> (*false* if *a* is *true*, else *true*)

The tilde symbol (~) is equivalent to NOT and the ampersand symbol (&) is equivalent to AND.

The operators AND and OR are defined in such a way that the second operand is only evaluated if the result cannot be determined from the first operand alone. Thus in expressions such as

        (index < indexMax) AND (arrayVar[index] = 0)

the first term can be used to ensure that the second term is only evaluated when it is safe to do so. In this example, arrayVar is only accessed when the value of index is within the allowed range of index values.

2.2.2 Type CARDINAL

The domain of this type consists of the positive integers (ie. 0, 1, 2, 3 etc.). [In practice, the domain always has an upper limit determined by the implementation. Its value is given by MAX(CARDINAL) <see **Standard Procedures**, p.92>. An attempt to create a value outside the allowed range produces an error; with a running program this usually causes it to fail.]

CARDINAL literals can take three forms, allowing values to be represented as decimal, octal or hexadecimal numbers:

> *digit* { *digit* }   (decimal format)
> *octdigit* { *octdigit* } B   (octal format)
> *digit* { *hexdigit* } H   (hexadecimal format)

where *digit* is a character in the range 0 to 9, *octdigit* is a character in the range 0 to 7, and *hexdigit* is a decimal digit or an upper-case letter in the range A to F. The following shows an example of each of these forms:

        2713   5231B   0A99H

9

(In fact all three represent the same value.) The hexadecimal form must begin with a decimal digit in order that numbers can be differentiated from identifiers; if the first character would otherwise be a letter, a zero digit should be be added at the beginning, as shown in the third example.

The CARDINAL operations are:

+	addition	($a + b$ and also $+a$)
−	subtraction	($a - b$ and also $-a$)
*	multiplication	($a * b$)
DIV	division with truncation	(a DIV b)
MOD	remainder of division	(a MOD b)

For example, the following CARDINAL division and remainder expressions produce the results shown:

5 DIV 3	->	1
3 DIV 5	->	0
5 MOD 3	->	2
3 MOD 5	->	3

[Some implementations provide an additional type, LONGCARD, which is identical to CARDINAL except that it has a larger domain. LONGCARD is usually assignment-compatible with types CARDINAL, INTEGER and LONGINT.]

2.2.3 Type CHAR

The domain of this type consists of the sequence of characters provided by the implementation. No general assumptions should be made about the particular characters provided, or their ordering, except than that the domain will at least include the basis character set <see **Basis character set**, p.1>. Many more characters than this are usually available, however. [Strictly, it is not even safe to assume that the alphabetic characters are arranged in normal alphabetic order, or to assume any particular relative ordering between lower-case and upper-case letters. Nevertheless, the character set almost universally encountered in practice is the ISO/ASCII one <see **Appendix 1**, p.108>. Implementation documentation should be consulted if there is any doubt about the actual set provided.]

10

Character literal constants can be represented in two forms. The first form is a single-character string literal, since this is assignment-compatible with type CHAR <see **Array type**, p.23>:

> " *character* "   or   ' *character* '

where *character* can be any (printable) character other than the particular enclosing quote symbol used.
   Examples of such single-character string literals are:

   "a"   '8'   "!"   '@'   "@"   " ' "   ' " '

(The last two examples represent the single and double quote characters respectively.)
   The above form is the one most frequently used, because it represents characters directly. However, it is not suitable for non-printable characters (eg. control characters). The second representation, although less convenient for normal characters, can be used to represent all available characters, including the non-printable ones. It has the form:

> *octdigit* { *octdigit* } c

Each *octdigit* is a digit in the range 0 to 7. The character represented is the one whose ordinal number (ie. position in the character sequence) is given by the octal value formed from the digits. [The actual character obtained is determined by the implementation; for example, with the ISO/ASCII character set, the literal constant 40c represents the space character and 141c represents the lower-case letter a.]
   No character operations as such are provided. However, the standard procedures CHR and ORD make it possible to convert an ordinal number into a character and vice-versa. Lower-case letters can be converted into upper-case ones using the standard procedure CAP <see **Value-returning procedures**, p.91>.

2.2.4 Type INTEGER
   This type is similar to CARDINAL, but with a domain consisting of signed values. [As with CARDINAL, the domain is limited in practice; values must be in the (inclusive) range MIN(INTEGER)

to MAX(INTEGER) <see **Value-returning procedures**, p.92>. An attempt to create a value outside the allowed range produces an error; with a running program this usually causes it to fail.]

INTEGER literal constants have the same form as CARDINAL ones <see above>, and therefore signed INTEGER literal constants are not available as such. However, a simple expression (eg. -100 or +35) can be used to denote a signed value, because an expression can appear anywhere that a literal constant is allowed.

The operations provided are the same as those of CARDINAL <see above>. With multiplication and division, opposite signs cancel in the usual way. However, the result of MOD is not defined when any operand is negative. For example, the following expressions produce the results shown:

```
-5 DIV  3   ->              -1
 5 DIV -3   ->              -1
-5 DIV -3   ->              +1
-5 MOD  3   ->         undefined
```

[Some implementations provide an additional type, LONGINT, which is identical to INTEGER except that it has a larger domain. LONGINT is usually assignment-compatible with types CARDINAL, INTEGER and LONGCARD.]

2.2.5 Type REAL

The domain of this type consists of the real numbers. [In practice, it is restricted in two ways. Firstly, the magnitude of a REAL value is limited; a typical largest magnitude is $\sim 10^{+38}$ and a typical smallest non-zero magnitude is $\sim 10^{-39}$. Secondly, its precision is also limited; an accuracy of 7 or 14 decimal digits is typical. An attempt to create a value whose magnitude is larger than the maximum produces an error; with a running program this usually causes it to fail. On the other hand, an attempt to create a value whose magnitude is less than the smallest non-zero magnitude usually results in the number being rounded to zero rather than causing a serious error; in the case of a running program, execution continues undisturbed.]

Literal constants of type REAL have the form:

> *digit* { *digit* } . { *digit* } [*exponent*]

12

where the optional *exponent* has the form

>   E [*sign*] *digit* { *digit* }

The optional *sign* is either the + or - character, while *digit* is any character in the range 0 to 9. Note that the minimum requirement for a REAL literal constant is one digit followed by a decimal point.
Examples of REAL literal constants are:

     0.5   3.   1.0E-24   1.E4   3.14159

Signed REAL literal constants are not available as such. However, a simple expression (eg. -0.5 or +59.6) can be used to denote a signed value, because an expression can appear anywhere that a literal constant is allowed.
The REAL operators are:

+	addition	($a + b$ and also $+a$)
-	subtraction	($a - b$ and also $-a$)
*	multiplication	($a * b$)
/	division	(a / b)

[Some implementations provide an additional type, LONGREAL, which is identical to REAL except that it provides greater precision and/or a wider range of values. LONGREAL is usually assignment-compatible with type REAL.]

2.3 User-defined types
The range of types available is not restricted to a fixed set of standard types; new application-specific types can be created as required by means of the following user-defined types:

- enumerated type
- subrange type
- set type
- record type
- array type
- pointer type
- procedure type

13

Each of these is a type class rather than a specific type, and acts as a template with particular characteristic properties from which specific types can be created as required. These different type classes are described in the following sections.

2.3.1 Enumerated type

This provides types whose domain is directly specified as an ordered sequence of values. The form of the type definition is

> (*ident* { , *ident* })

where each *ident* is an identifier defining a literal constant and hence also a value of the type. Because the sequence is ordered, each value has a corresponding *ordinal number*, ie. a position in the sequence. Standard type BOOLEAN is in fact an example of an enumerated type; the literals FALSE and TRUE have the respective ordinal numbers 0 and 1.

The following type declaration contains various enumerated type definitions:

```
TYPE
    Day          = (mon,tue,wed,thu,fri,sat,sun);
    Month        = (jan,feb,mar,apr,may,jun,
                    jul,aug,sep,oct,nov,dec);
    Direction    = (north,south,east,west);
    Weather      = (rainy,cloudy,bright,sunny);
    TrafficLight = (red,amber,green);
    RomanNumber  = (I,II,III,IV,V,VI,VII,VIII,IX,X);
```

For example, the ordinal numbers of sun and mon (of type Day) are 6 and 0 respectively.

Literal constants of enumerated types automatically have the same scope as the parent type name. They must be unique in that scope, since otherwise an ambiguity would exist. If the same literal is used by more than one enumerated type and the scopes of the types overlap, a name-clash error will occur. This kind of error can be hard to track down, because the relevant identifiers only appear in type definitions that are generally nowhere near the position of the error. If the definitions are in standard global modules, it will almost certainly not be possible to change them unilaterally. Literal constants of enumerated types should therefore always be chosen so that they are likely to remain unique. For example, the enumerated-type definition

(ready,busy,error)

defines values which are too general for (say) the status of a disc drive. A better choice would be a definition such as:

(driveReady,driveBusy,driveError)

No operations are provided for user-defined enumerated types. However, an enumerated value can be converted into the equivalent ordinal number using the standard procedure ORD, and an ordinal number can be converted into the equivalent value of any required enumerated type using the standard procedure VAL <see **Value-returning procedures**, p.92 & p.93>.

2.3.2 Subrange type

This allows a new type to be defined which is essentially the same as an existing type (the *base type*) but with a more restricted domain of values. The definition has the form:

> [*typeIdent*] [*constExpression* .. *constExpression*]

The identifier *typeIdent*, which can be a qualified identifier, indicates the required base type. This can be any standard type (except REAL), any enumerated type, or any subrange type. Each *constExpression* must be a constant expression of the base type, and the second expression must have a value greater than the first. The domain of the new type consists of all values (inclusive) between the given limits.

The type identifier can be omitted only if the base type can be derived unambiguously from the expressions. If both values are positive integers, the base type is taken to be CARDINAL; if one or both is a negative integer, the base type is INTEGER.

The following declaration defines a number of subrange types:

```
TYPE
    Digit    = ["0" .. "9"];      (* base type CHAR.  *)
    WeekDay  = [mon .. fri];      (* base type Day.   *)
    WeekEnd  = Day[sat .. sun];   (*    - ditto -     *)
    Byte     = [0 .. 255];        (* base CARDINAL.   *)
    SmallInt = [-10 .. +10];      (* base INTEGER.    *)
    TenScale = Dial.Scale[0..10]; (* via module Dial.*)
```

The literal constants and operators of the subrange type are inherited from the base type. The base type and the subrange type are compatible, so no conversion is needed between values of the two types. However, valid values of the base type are not necessarily valid values of the subrange type because of the latter's smaller domain.

2.3.3 Set type

This allows a type to be created whose domain consists of all sets which can be constructed from the values of a given base type. The form of a set type definition is:

> SET OF *typeDesc*

The base type is given by *typeDesc*, which is either a type identifier or a type definition. A type identifier can be qualified. The base type can be any enumerated type, any subrange of an enumerated type, or a subrange of CARDINAL or INTEGER.

For example, the types defined by

```
TYPE
    BoolSet   =  SET OF BOOLEAN;
    Triplet   =  SET OF [0..2];
    DecSet    =  SET OF [0..9];
```

have domains consisting of the following set values:

BoolSet: { }, {false}, {true}, {false, true}
Triplet: { }, {0}, {1}, {2}, {0,1}, {0,2}, {1,2}, {0,1,2}
DecSet: all 1024 possible sets of integers 0 to 9.

The empty set { } is a value of every set type.

[Unfortunately, no minimum requirement exists for the size of set which must be supported by an implementation. Some implementations consequently put rather severe restrictions on the set size, and hence on the number of values allowed in the base type's domain. A maximum of 16 or 32 values is not unusual. This somewhat limits the usefulness of set types. For example, the above set type DecSet might not be acceptable to all implementations. The potentially very useful type SET OF CHAR is often not allowed either.]

16

Set literal constants have the following form:

>   [*typeIdent*] { [*elementRange* (, *elementRange* }] }

The identifier *typeIdent*, which can be qualified, indicates the value's type; this must be the name of an existing set type. Each *elementRange* has the form:

>   *expression* [.. *expression*]

If a single expression is given, a single element value is specified; if a pair of expressions are given, all element values (inclusive) between the specified values are included. The expressions need not be constant expressions. [However, such a restriction is sometimes imposed by older implementations.] All expressions must be of the base type of the set.

For example, the literal constants

    DecSet{0,1,2,3,5,9}   and   DecSet{0..3,5,9}

both represent the same value of the set type DecSet. If the type name is omitted, the base type BITSET is assumed <see **Type BITSET**, p.79>.

Four set operations are provided:

+	set union	($a + b$)
–	ordered set difference	($a - b$)
*	set intersection	($a * b$)
/	symmetric set difference	(a / b)

For example, if set01 and set12 are variables of the set type Triplet, and have the values *Triplet{0,1}* and *Triplet{1,2}* respectively, the following expressions produce the results shown:

set01 + set12	->	*Triplet{0,1,2}*
set01 - set12	->	*Triplet{0}*
set12 - set01	->	*Triplet{2}*
set01 * set12	->	*Triplet{1}*
set01 / set12	->	*Triplet{0,2}*

Additionally, the operator IN can be used to determine whether a particular element is contained within a given set or not. It appears in an expression of the form:

>   *value* IN *setValue*

The type of *value* must be compatible with the base type of the set value used. The result is a BOOLEAN value which is *true* if the element is in the set and *false* otherwise.

For example, with the following expressions involving the set type Triplet, the results are:

```
3 IN Triplet{1,2,3}  ->    true
3 IN Triplet{2,4,8}  ->    false
```

In general, such expressions can contain element and set variables as well as literal constants, if required.

Relational operators can be used to test for set equality and inclusion <see **Relational operators**, p.29>, and the standard procedures INCL and EXCL are available to add and remove single elements from a set <see **Proper procedures**, p.89 & p.90>.

2.3.4 Record type

This enables a type to be defined as a collection of components of various other available types (standard types and/or user-defined ones). Each component of a record is known as a *field*. The form of a record type definition is:

>   RECORD *fieldDefinition* { ; *fieldDefinition* } END

Each *fieldDefinition* defines a particular field, and has two possible forms, depending on whether the field is to have a unique structure (a *fixed field*) or a number of alternative structures (a *variant field*).

a) Fixed field

A fixed field definition is used to specify a field which has only one possible structure. It has the following form:

>   [*ident* { , *ident* } : *typeDesc*]

18

Each *ident* specifies the name of a field. This must be unique within the record. The list of field names is followed by *typeDesc* which specifies the type of the fields; this can be a type identifier indicating an existing type or alternatively a new type definition. The type identifier can be a qualified identifier, so that type names from other modules can be used.

(The definition allows a completely null field; this is merely so that some trivial compilation errors are avoided.)

The following is an example of a type declaration which defines a record type with three fixed fields:

```
TYPE
   Time = RECORD
             hour       : [0 .. 23];
             min, sec   : [0 .. 59]
          END
```

Records of type Time thus have the fields hour, min, sec, the type of each being an appropriate subrange of CARDINAL.

b) Variant field

A variant field definition is used to specify a field which can have alternative structures. It consists of a list of definitions together with a special field (the *tag field* or *discriminant*) which makes it possible for a program to set the current variant of any variable of this record type at run-time. The form of a variant field definition is:

> [CASE [*tagIdent*] : *tagTypeIdent* OF
>   *variantDefinition* { | *variantDefinition* }
>   [ELSE *fieldDefinition* { ; *fieldDefinition* }] END]

The type of the tag field is given by *tagTypeIdent*, which can be any existing type name. It can be a qualified identifier. The type must be an enumerated type, CARDINAL, INTEGER, CHAR or any subrange of these. The (optional) tag field is specified by *tagIdent*. (A tag field can be very useful. If a variant-record variable has a tag field, the current variant can be set explicitly by assigning an appropriate value to its tag field, and the variant which the variable currently possesses can be found by examining its tag field. On the other hand, if the variable has no

19

tag field, the current variant cannot be set explicitly, and the variant which the variable currently possesses cannot be determined directly. Other, less direct, means must then be used to keep track of the current variant.)

Each *variantDefinition* defines one of the available structures, and has the form:

>   [*caseRange* { , *caseRange* } : *fieldDefinition*]

Each *fieldDefinition* is a normal field definition, and can therefore also be fixed or variant. (Thus, variants within variants within... etc., are possible).

Within each variant definition, *caseRange* specifies the value (or values) of the tag which will select that particular variant. It has the form:

>   *constExpression* [.. *constExpression*]

A single value is specified by a single expression, and a range of values (inclusive) by two expressions. The second expression (if used) should have a value greater than the first. The case ranges of different variants should not overlap, since this would produce an ambiguity.

If the optional ELSE part is included, this variant is selected if the tag value lies outside the ranges of all the other variants.

As an example, the following declaration creates a record type with one fixed field and one variant field (the latter having a tag field):

```
TYPE
    Airports    = (abz,ams,beo,bru,cdg,gla); (*etc.*)
    PlaneTypes  = (ab3,b57,dc9,emb,f50);     (*etc.*)
    Plane       = RECORD
                    planeType  : PlaneTypes;
                    CASE inAir : BOOLEAN OF
                      FALSE :
                        airport : Airports;
                        gate    : [1..500]    |
                      TRUE :
                        height  : [0..50000]
                    END (*CASE*)
                  END (*RECORD*)
```

Variables of type Plane therefore have three or four fields, namely the fixed field planeType, the tag field inAir, and either the field height (if inAir is *true*) or the fields airport and gate (if inAir is *false*).

[With most implementations, the amount of memory allocated to a variable of a particular record type is usually constant, and is enough to hold the largest possible variant. Attempts to save memory by defining large, infrequently-used fields as variant fields therefore do not usually succeed; on the contrary, slightly more space may be needed to hold any additional tag field(s).]

The fields of a given record can be of any type except that of the same record; ie. directly self-recursive record definitions are not allowed. However, a record type xyz can have fields of type POINTER TO xyz <see **Pointer type**, p.24>.

Unfortunately, literal constants of record types are not provided, so there is no way to assign a constant record value to a record variable directly; the variable can only be set field-by-field. Also, an actual procedure parameter of any record type must always be a variable. However, the value of a record variable (whether fixed or variant) can be directly assigned to any variable of the same type <see **Assignment**, p.41>.

No record operators are provided. Any required field of a record variable can be accessed individually via a *record field selector*. This consists of a period character followed by the field name, and appears in an expression of the following form:

> *varIdent* { *selector* } . *fieldIdent*

The field name is given by *fieldIdent*. The part before the selector should indicate a record variable (or record component of a variable) of the correct type. It consists of the variable name *varIdent* (which may be a qualified identifier) followed by any suitable sequence of record field selectors, array element selectors and pointer dereferences. Usually it will simply be the name of a record variable.

For example, if myPlane is a variable of the above record type Plane, then its fields can be accessed by statements such as

```
myPlane.planeType:= f50;
myPlane.inAir:= TRUE;
IF (myPlane.inAir) THEN myPlane.height:= 5000 END;
```

21

Similarly, if a fleet of aircraft is created by

```
VAR
    fleet : ARRAY [1..20] OF POINTER TO Plane;
```

then the characteristics of the fifth aircraft (say) of the fleet can be set by statements such as

```
fleet[5]^.planeType:=    f50;
fleet[5]^.inAir:=        TRUE;
fleet[5]^.height:=       8000
```

The field names of a record type automatically have the same scope as the parent type name.

2.3.5 Array type

Array types consist of an ordered collection of values of a single specified *base type*. The individual values (known as *array elements*) are dynamically accessible. The form of an array type definition is:

>   ARRAY *typeDesc* { , *typeDesc* } OF *baseTypeDesc*

Both *typeDesc* and *baseTypeDesc* are type identifiers or type definitions. Type identifiers can be qualified. The base type of the array is defined by *baseTypeDesc*. Each dimension of the array is defined by a separate *typeDesc*, which indicates the type of value (the *index type*) used to access the array in that dimension. The size of the array in any dimension is set by the number of values in the domain of the corresponding index type. Index types are restricted to being enumerated types, CHAR, and subranges of these or of CARDINAL and INTEGER. The index type(s) are part of the array type, so array types with different index types (even if the latter are only different ranges of the same original type) are not type-compatible.

As an example, the following type declaration

```
TYPE
    Single     = ARRAY [-5..5] OF REAL;
    Double     = ARRAY BOOLEAN,["a".."z"] OF INTEGER;
```

defines two array types. The first is a one-dimensional array of

22

11 REAL elements whose index type is a subrange of INTEGER. The second is a two-dimensional array of 2 x 26 INTEGER elements; its first dimension is indexed by a BOOLEAN value (ie. *true/false*) and its second by a character value in the range "a" to "z".

Except for one special case, no literal constants of array types are possible. The exception is for values of type ARRAY [0..m] OF CHAR (where m is a positive integer constant), known as *character strings*. These have literal constants with either of the following two forms:

> " { *char* } "   (ie. using double quotes)

> ' { *char* } '   (ie. using single quotes)

where each *char* is any single representable character other than the enclosing quote symbol.

Examples of character-string literal constants are:

```
"a string"    'more than one character'    "it's"
```

The type of a string literal of length n characters is ARRAY [0..(n-1)] OF CHAR. It is possible to assign a string literal to a character-string variable which has a larger upper bound, in which case a null character [value *0C* in the ISO/ASCII set] is appended. A single-character string literal is also assignment-compatible with type CHAR ‹see **Type CHAR**, p.10›. [However, this might not be allowed by some older implementations.]

No array operations are provided. An array variable can be accessed as a whole, for example in an assignment statement. Any particular element of an array variable can also be accessed individually via an *array element selector*. This consists of a sequence of expressions in square brackets, each expression giving a suitable value of the relevant index type. This appears in an expression which has either of the following forms:

> *varIdent* { *selector* } [*expression* { , *expression* }]

> *varIdent* { *selector* } [*expression*] { [*expression*] }

The part which precedes the array element selector should

indicate an array variable (or array component of a variable) of the correct type. It consists of the variable name *varIdent* (which can be a qualified identifier) followed by any suitable sequence of record field selectors, array element selectors and pointer dereferences. Usually it is simply the name of an array variable.

There should be as many expressions in the selector as there are array dimensions, and each expression should be compatible with the type of the corresponding index. Thus, if singleVar and doubleVar are respectively variables of the array types Single and Double defined above, the following assignments are valid:

```
singleVar[index]      :=  9.5;
doubleVar[TRUE,"c"]   :=  doubleVar[FALSE]["r"];
doubleVar[TRUE]["c"]  :=  -20
```

A means is provided of allowing a procedure to define array formal parameters without specifying their index types. This allows the procedure to accept arrays of different sizes and/or index types <see **Open-array parameters**, p.56>.

2.3.6 Pointer type
A value of this type is a reference to a variable of a specified type. The form of a pointer type definition is

>   POINTER TO *typeDesc*

where *typeDesc* is a type identifier or a type definition, and specifies the type of variable which the pointer type can reference. A type identifier can be a qualified identifier.

For example, with the type declaration

```
TYPE
   IntPointer         =  POINTER TO INTEGER;
   IntPointerPointer  =  POINTER TO IntPointer;
```

a value of type IntPointer is a reference to an INTEGER variable, and a value of type IntPointerPointer is a reference to a variable of type IntPointer.

One literal constant of this type is provided. This is the predefined identifier NIL, whose value is *no location* (*nil*). This

24

value is compatible with any pointer type. Other pointer values are typically created when memory is allocated to (anonymous) variables using (for example) the procedure ALLOCATE exported from the standard module Storage <see **Standard Modules,** p.102>. For example, with the variable intPoint of type IntPointer, a new (anonymous) INTEGER variable, referenced by intPoint, is created by the statement

```
ALLOCATE(intPoint,TSIZE(INTEGER))
```

[Pointer values can also be created by obtaining references to existing (named) variables using the procedure ADR, and can be calculated using values of types such as ADDRESS; however, a sound understanding of the particular implementation is essential if such methods are to succeed. They are usually only necessary in special cases such as systems programming <see **Low-Level Facilities,** p.77>.]

The variable referenced by a pointer variable is accessed by means of a *pointer dereference*. This is represented by an uparrow (^) character, and appears in an expression of the following form:

> *varIdent { selector } ^*

The part before the dereference symbol should indicate a pointer variable (or pointer component of a variable) of the correct type. It consists of the variable name *varIdent* (which may be a qualified identifier) followed by any suitable sequence of record field selectors, array element selectors and pointer dereferences. Most often it is simply the name of a pointer variable.

For example, if the variable intPoint is of type POINTER TO INTEGER, a value can be assigned to the variable referenced by intPoint (provided one exists), and the value of this variable can be accessed (here it is copied to the integer variable int) by statements such as

```
intPoint^:= -10;
int := intPoint^
```

25

An attempt to dereference the value *nil* causes an error, since no referenced variable exists in this case. [Such an error will usually cause a program to fail.] If the variable intPoint (say) could have the value *nil*, failure is avoided by use of conditional dereferences such as:

```
IF (intPoint # NIL) THEN intPoint^:= -10 END
```

Used in conjunction with other types (especially records), pointers make it possible to construct useful dynamic data structures such as linked lists and binary trees.

2.3.7 Procedure type

The procedure is not only the means by which particular named actions are declared <see **Procedures**, p.53>, it is also a distinct type class. Although procedure values cannot be calculated by expressions, they can be passed as parameters and saved in (procedure) variables in exactly the same way as values of other types. Like a declared procedure, the procedure value stored in a variable can be called on to perform whatever action it implements, <see **Procedure calls**, p.48>. The form of a procedure type definition is:

> PROCEDURE [([*paramDef* { , *paramDef* }])
> [: *typeIdent*]]

The identifier *typeIdent*, if present, indicates that a value is returned and also specifies its type; it can be a qualified identifier. The return type can be any type other than a set, record, array or procedure type. Each *paramDef* defines a separate parameter, and has the form

> [VAR] [ARRAY OF] *typeIdent*

where *typeIdent* is an identifier which specifies the type of the parameter. It can be a qualified identifier.

If the symbol VAR is omitted, the parameter is a value parameter; if it is included, the parameter is a variable parameter <see **Procedure parameters**, p.54>. The optional phrase ARRAY OF is used to indicate an open-array parameter

26

<see **Open-array parameters**, p.56>.

Parameter brackets are obligatory if the procedure is a value-returning procedure; if the procedure requires no parameters, the brackets will be empty.

Examples of procedure-type definitions are:

```
TYPE
    Proc1  = PROCEDURE (CARDINAL, REAL, VAR INTEGER);
    Proc2  = PROCEDURE ( ): CHAR;
    Proc3  = PROCEDURE;
    Proc4  = PROCEDURE (VAR ARRAY OF REAL);
```

The predefined identifier PROC represents a parameterless procedure which does not return a value (ie. PROC = PROCEDURE).

Any procedure name defined by a procedure declaration <see **Procedure declarations**, p.35> can be regarded as a manifest constant of procedure type, and can be used as a procedure value. In such a case, however, the declaration must not be local to any other procedure. A standard procedure cannot be used as a procedure value. (However, a new procedure can be created which has the same parameters as the standard procedure and which simply calls the latter; this new procedure can be used in place of the standard one).

2.4 Type compatibility

Types are *compatible* if their values can be freely mixed in expressions and assigned to variables of any of the types. In Modula, two types are compatible (a) if one is a subrange of the other, (b) if both are subranges of the same parent type, or (c) if one is defined directly from another type. However, if types are defined independently, they are not considered to be compatible, even if they have identical structures. For example, with the following declaration

```
TYPE
    Pos    = RECORD x, y : REAL  END;
    Size   = RECORD x, y : REAL  END;
    Coord  = Pos;
```

the types Pos and Coord are compatible, but neither of them is compatible with type Size.

A slightly more relaxed form of compatibility is used in

27

assignments <see **Assignment**, p.40>.

Note that, although they have much in common, types INTEGER and CARDINAL are not compatible; for example, if variables intVar and cardVar are respectively of types INTEGER and CARDINAL, the expression

intVar + cardVar

is not valid. One of the values must be converted into a value of the other type. [(This also applies to expressions containing any mix of CARDINAL, INTEGER, LONGCARD and LONGINT values, if the latter types are also available.)

Sometimes the conversion can be done by means of a type transfer, as in the expression

intVar + INTEGER(cardVar)

although this does not always achieve the desired effect <see **Type transfer**, p.77>.]

However, the types INTEGER and CARDINAL are assignment-compatible, so an INTEGER value can be assigned to a CARDINAL variable (or vice-versa), provided the value is within the domain of the variable's type. Thus the statement

cardVar := intVar

is allowed. Nevertheless, an error will occur if the value of intVar is outside the domain of CARDINAL (if the value is negative, for example). [(The same applies to values of type LONGCARD and LONGINT.) Such an error might possibly produce a spurious value rather than causing the program to fail.]

Values of type INTEGER and CARDINAL are neither type nor assignment compatible with those of type REAL, and type transfer will not perform a true type conversion. However, correct conversion between CARDINAL and REAL is possible using the standard procedures FLOAT and TRUNC <see **Value-returning procedures**, p.91 & p.93>, while conversion between INTEGER and REAL is usually available by means of the procedures entier and real exported from the module MathLib <see **Standard Modules**, p.100>. Thus, for example, if cardVar and realVar are

28

variables of type CARDINAL and REAL respectively, the following expressions are all type-compatible:

FLOAT(cardVar)/realVar

FLOAT(cardVar DIV 2)

TRUNC(realVar) DIV cardVar

(The first two expressions are of type REAL and the third is of type CARDINAL.)

[If the types LONGCARD and LONGREAL are available, equivalent conversions between them may well be possible using standard procedures TRUNCD and FLOATD.]

2.5 Relational operators

Two values of the same type can be compared using a *relational expression*. Such an expression has the form:

> *value relOperator value*

where the two values are of the same type (or of compatible types) and *relOperator* is one of the available relational operators. The result is of type BOOLEAN, being *true* if the given relation is correct, and *false* otherwise. The operators are:

=	"equal to"	
#	"not equal to"	(equivalent to <>)
<>	"not equal to"	(equivalent to #)
<	"less than"	(for sets: "included in")
>	"greater than"	(for sets: "includes")
<=	"less than or equal to"	
>=	"greater than or equal to"	

Relational operators can be used with values of any enumerated type, CARDINAL, INTEGER, REAL, CHAR, or any subrange of these. The equality and inequality operators can also be used with pointer and set values; the operators < and > are valid for sets, and test for set inclusion as indicated above.

For enumerated types, a value with a smaller ordinal number is less than one with a larger ordinal number. [The ordering of

29

characters (ie. values of type CHAR) is implementation-dependent, since it depends on the actual character set used.]
For example, the following expressions give the results shown:

5 = 3	->	*false*
5 # 3	->	*true*
TRUE > FALSE	->	*true*
{1,2} = {1,2,3}	->	*false*
{1,2} < {1,2,3}	->	*true*

2.6 Operator precedence

For programming convenience, all the available operators obey certain precedence rules. They are divided into four precedence classes as follows:

1:	NOT	~				
2:	*	/	DIV	AND	&	MOD
3:	+	-	OR			
4:	=	#	<>	<	>	<=	>=	IN

Class 1 has the highest precedence and class 4 the lowest. Where operators in an expression are in the same class, the precedence is from left to right. The default precedences can be overridden by using round brackets, when required.
For example, the following expressions produce the results shown:

2 * 3 + 4	->	*10*	(ie. = 6 + 4)
2 * (3 + 4)	->	*14*	(ie. = 2 * 7)
2 * 3 DIV 4	->	*1*	(ie. = 6 DIV 4)
2 * (3 DIV 4)	->	*0*	(ie. = 2 * 0)

Note that all relational operators have a lower precedence than logical operators, so brackets are essential in a BOOLEAN expression such as

(value1 < value2) AND (value3 = value4)

since without them the expression is equivalent to

(value1 < (value2 AND value3)) = value4

30

The second expression not only has a radically different
meaning, it is in fact only valid when the values all happen to be
of type BOOLEAN.

3 Declarations

3.1 General

All identifiers used in a module or procedure (apart from the reserved words and the predefined identifiers) must be defined somewhere, whether locally or (if imported from another module) in that module. The establishing of definitions for identifiers is done by *declarations*. All declarations in a module or procedure must precede the statement sequence. Five kinds of declaration are available:

- TYPE — defines type names
- CONST — defines manifest constants
- VAR — defines named variables
- PROCEDURE — defines named procedures
- MODULE — defines local modules

These are described in the following sections.

3.2 Type declarations

A type declaration defines identifiers which are to be used as type names. It has the following form:

> TYPE { *ident* = *typeDesc* ; }

Each *ident* specifies the name of the new type, and each *typeDesc* is either an existing type identifier or a new type definition.

An existing type identifier indicates the type on which the new one is based. It can be a qualified identifier. For example, the declaration

```
TYPE
    MyCard   = CARDINAL;
    MyColour = Lights.Colour;
```

creates a new type called MyCard which has the same properties as CARDINAL, and another called MyColour which has the same properties as the type Colour exported from the module Lights. The new type and the existing type are type-compatible. The existing type can be a standard type or another user-defined one.

The more common alternative is to use a new type definition. This enables a new type to be constructed from a suitable combination of existing types, which can be other user-defined types as well as standard ones. Several kinds of type definition are available <see **User-defined types**, p.13>. As an example, the following declaration creates seven new types, each of which is created using one of the available type definitions:

```
TYPE
   SubRange    = [-1..+1];
   Enumeration = (one,two,three,four,five,six,seven);
   Set         = SET OF Enumeration;
   Record      = RECORD
                    first  : CARDINAL;
                    second : SubRange;
                    third  : CHAR
                 END;
   Array       = ARRAY INTEGER,SubRange OF Record;
   Pointer     = POINTER TO Record;
   Procedure   = PROCEDURE(REAL,Set) : SubRange;
```

3.3 Constant declarations

Constant declarations allow identifiers to be defined as *manifest constants*, ie. where each identifier represents a particular fixed value. The form of a constant declaration is

> CONST { *ident = constExpression ; }

Each *ident* specifies the name of the new constant, and each *constExpression* is a constant expression which gives its value.

For example, the following constant declaration defines two constants of type REAL:

```
CONST
   pi    = 3.141593;
   twopi = 2.0 * pi;
```

A manifest constant is particularly useful when the same fixed value is used a number of times in various places in a section of code. Without it, a literal constant would have to be used, and since it is repeated numerous times, there is some possibility that the value would be mistyped at least once. Even worse, if it ever becomes necessary to change the value, every instance of the literal constant in the code has to be found and amended. If even a single amendment is made incorrectly, or omitted, an error will be introduced. However, if a manifest constant is used instead, the compiler will usually detect any mistyped identifier (provided all identifiers are sufficiently distinct), and its value can be changed easily and safely by amending a single constant declaration.

3.4 Variable declarations

Named variables are defined using declarations of the form:

> VAR { *ident* { , *ident* } : *typeDesc* ; }

Each *ident* specifies the name of the new variable. Every list of names is followed by *typeDesc* which specifies the type of the variables in the list. This type description can be either an existing type identifier or a new type definition. A type identifier can be a qualified identifier, so that type names from other modules can be used if required. A type definition can be any of those available <see **User-defined types**, p.13>.

For example, the variable declaration

```
VAR
    intVar1,intVar2    : INTEGER;
    myVar              : MyType;
    light1,light2      : (red,amber,green);
```

creates two variables of standard type INTEGER, one variable of the user-defined type MyType, and two of a newly-defined (unnamed) enumerated type.

Note that variables declared using a new type definition (such as light1 and light2 above) are only type-compatible with other variables declared in the same variable list. They are not type-compatible with variables declared elsewhere, even within the same declaration. This is true even if the definitions are identical. However, variables are always type-compatible if they are declared using the same type name. It is therefore good

34

practice to name all types explicitly (using type declarations) and then declare variables using only the type names.

[In some implementations, variables can be placed at given memory addresses <see **Absolute-address variables**, p.78>. The address of any named variable can be found using the procedure ADR, which is exported from the special module SYSTEM <see **Memory-enquiry procedures**, p.81>.]

3.5 Procedure declarations

A procedure declaration allows an identifier to be defined as representing a particular statement sequence. The statement sequence is executed when a statement formed from this identifier is executed; this is known as *calling* the procedure <see **Procedure calls**, p.48>.

Since a procedure is a value of a distinct type <see **Procedure type**, p.26>, a procedure declaration can also be thought of as a special constant declaration which names a value of a particular procedure type. This value can be assigned, if required, to procedure variables of that type.

The form of a procedure declaration is:

> PROCEDURE *ident* [([*paramDef* { ; *paramDef* }])
>   [: *typeIdent*]] ;
>   { *declaration* ; }
>   BEGIN *statement* { ; *statement* } END *ident* ;

where *ident* is the identifier which defines the procedure name. (Note that it is given twice, at the beginning and also at the end.) Each *paramDef* defines one or more procedure parameters.

If present, the type identifier *typeIdent* indicates that the procedure returns a value of the given type. This may be any type other than a set, record, array or procedure type. The type identifier can be qualified. This kind of procedure is known as a *value-returning procedure*, and is always called by means of an expression <see **Procedure calls**, p.48>. The brackets are obligatory in the declaration of a value-returning procedure, and will be empty if the procedure has no parameters. If *typeIdent* is not present, the procedure does not return a value. This kind of procedure is known as a *proper procedure*, and is always called by means of a (unique) statement.

35

Each *declaration* enables local types, constants, variables, procedures or modules to be defined within the procedure.

The procedure is an important construct, and is described in greater detail in a later chapter <see **Procedures**, p.53>.

3.6 Module declarations

A module declaration allows a named region of code to be defined which can be isolated in a very controlled way from the surrounding code. It is a local version of a much more general construct. A module declaration has the following form:

> MODULE *ident* [[*constExpression*]] ;
> { *importClause* }
> [*exportClause*]
> { *declaration* }
> [BEGIN *statement* { ; *statement* }] END *ident* ;

As with all kinds of module, the two occurrences of *ident* define the name of the module. The presence of *constExpression* within square brackets indicates that it is a monitor <see **Monitors**, p.72>. Each *importClause* specifies the identifiers available in the surrounding code which are also to be available inside the module, while the (single) *exportClause* specifies the identifiers available inside the module which are also to be available outside it. Each *declaration* is a standard declaration which defines local types, constants, variables, procedures or other local modules.

A local module can have its own statement sequence, which is placed between the BEGIN and END symbols. Unlike a procedure statement sequence, which is executed when the procedure is (explicitly) called, a local module statement sequence is executed automatically, and effectively acts as a prelude to the statement sequence of the procedure or module in which the local module is declared. A module statement sequence is usually used to initialise module local variables.

The local module is one instance of an important construct which is one of the major features of Modula, and which is described in greater detail in a later chapter <see **Modules**, p.59>.

36

3.7 Order of declarations

Declarations can occur in any order, subject to the following rules:

- identifiers used in a declaration must have been defined in a textually-preceding declaration or in an import clause.
- the above rule is relaxed slightly for pointer types. The definition POINTER TO SomeType can precede the actual declaration of SomeType, but both declarations must occur in the same module or procedure. [In many implementations, this also applies to procedure types, so that procedures can have (procedure) parameters which are mutually-referencing.]

For example, with the declaration

```
TYPE
    List     = POINTER TO ListNode;
    ListNode = RECORD
                  value : INTEGER;
                  next  : List
               END (*RECORD*);

    Scan     = PROCEDURE (Exec);
    Exec     = PROCEDURE (Scan);
```

the first pair of definitions is certainly valid. [The second pair is also accepted by many implementations.]

Note that although an identifier cannot be used in a declaration which precedes the one in which it is defined, it can be used in a **statement** which precedes the declaration. Thus (for example) the following code is correct:

```
PROCEDURE incVar;

BEGIN
    laterVar:= laterVar+1
END incVar;

VAR
    laterVar : CARDINAL; (* can be used above *)
```

3.8 Scope of definitions

Modules and procedures can include module and procedure declarations, which themselves can include more module and procedure declarations (etc.). This is known as *nesting*. Rules are provided so that, for an identifier defined at some particular point, the region of code within which that definition is valid can be determined. This is known as the *scope* of that definition of the identifier, or (for brevity) simply as the scope of the identifier. These rules are as follows:

- the scope of an identifier is (initially) the module or procedure within which it is declared.
- if the scope is a local module, the scope is extended by explicit export of the identifier to the module or procedure in which the local module is declared.
- if the scope is a definition module, the scope is extended to all program and global modules which explicitly import the identifier.
- the scope automatically includes all procedures contained within it, except for any procedures where the identifier is redefined (and all modules and procedures contained within them).
- the scope includes any (local) modules contained within it which import the identifier, but does not include those which do not (nor any modules or procedures contained within them).
- a predefined identifier is available everywhere except within modules or procedures where it is redefined.

The situation where a particular definition does not apply within an inner procedure (or module) because an identifier is redefined (or not imported), is known as a *hole-in-scope*.

Figure 3.1 illustrates the effect of the scope rules with nested procedures. The variable varB is visible everywhere, but its companion varA is not visible within any of the procedures because the identifier varA is redefined in outer. This is an example of a hole-in-scope. The identifier varD denotes a local CARDINAL variable in innerA and a different local BOOLEAN variable in innerB.

The means by which an identifier is exported from modules and imported into modules is described in the chapter on modules <see **Modules**, p.59>. This chapter also gives an example of a local module used to "hide" a shared variable <see **Module local variables**, p.74>.

```
MODULE ScopeEx;

    VAR varA,varB : INTEGER; (* --level 0 -- *)

    PROCEDURE outer;
        VAR varA,varC : CHAR;   (* --level 1 -- *)

        PROCEDURE innerA ;
            VAR varD : CARDINAL; (* --level 2a-- *)

        BEGIN (*innerA*) (* visible here are:
            innerA   PROCEDURE    level 1
            innerB   PROCEDURE    level 1
            outer    PROCEDURE    level 0
            varA     CHAR         level 1
            varB     INTEGER      level 0
            varC     CHAR         level 1
            varD     CARDINAL     level 2a
        END innerA;

        PROCEDURE innerB;
            VAR varD : BOOLEAN;  (* --level 2b-- *)

        BEGIN (*innerB*) (* visible here are:
            .. as for <innerA>,  except ..
            varD     BOOLEAN      level 2b *)
        END innerB;

    BEGIN (*outer*) (* visible here are:
        innerA   PROCEDURE    level 1
        innerB   PROCEDURE    level 1
        outer    PROCEDURE    level 0
        varA     CHAR         level 1
        varB     INTEGER      level 0
        varC     CHAR         level 1 *)
    END outer;

BEGIN (*ScopeEx*) (* visible here are:
    outer    PROCEDURE    level 0
    varA     INTEGER      level 0
    varB     INTEGER      level 0 *)
END ScopeEx.
```

Figure 3.1: Scope with nested procedures

4 Statements

4.1 General
Statements are the means by which all program actions are specified. They can be grouped into the following general categories:

- *assignment*- the saving of a value in a variable.
- *selection*- the choice between different actions:
     IF..THEN statement,
     CASE statement.
- *iteration*- the repetition of an action:
     WHILE..DO statement,
     REPEAT..UNTIL statement
     FOR..DO statement,
     LOOP and EXIT statements.
- *procedure call*- the execution of a named action.
- *miscellaneous*:
     RETURN statement,
     WITH..DO statement.

4.2 Assignment
This causes a new value to be assigned to a variable, and has the form:

> *varident* (*selector*) := *expression*

The part before the := symbol indicates the variable (or component of a variable) which is to be given the value provided by *expression*. Most often it is simply a variable name, but in general it can be a variable name followed by any appropriate sequence of record field selectors, array element selectors and pointer dereferences. The variable name can be a qualified identifier.

The types of the destination and the expression must be

assignment-compatible. This is a slightly relaxed form of type compatibility in which certain types are accepted as being equivalent for assignment purposes. CARDINAL, INTEGER, and subranges of these two types are assignment-compatible. A CARDINAL value can therefore be assigned to an INTEGER variable, and vice-versa. [If they are provided, LONGCARD and LONGINT are also assignment-compatible with these types. Type LONGREAL is also assignment-compatible with type REAL.] Note, however, that this does not guarantee that the assignment will succeed; for example, an attempt to assign a negative INTEGER value to a CARDINAL variable will certainly cause an error. This might cause the program to fail or (perhaps even worse) result in a spurious value being assigned.

Also, a character string can be assigned to a character-string variable of greater length, in which case a null character [*OC* in ISO/ASCII] is appended to the original string. Single-character strings are also assignment-compatible with type CHAR.

For example, with the variable declaration

```
VAR
    cardVar     : CARDINAL;
    intVar      : INTEGER;
    intArray1,
    intArray2   : ARRAY [1..5] OF INTEGER;
    point       : POINTER TO
                    ARRAY [1..10] OF
                      RECORD
                        field1: ARRAY[0..20] OF CHAR;
                        field2: INTEGER
                      END;
```

assignments such as the following are valid:

```
cardVar          := point^[1].field2 - 2*intVar
intArray1[3]     := intArray1[1];
intArray1        := intArray2
point^[4].field1 := "a"
```

In the first statement, the expression type is INTEGER, which is assignment-compatible with the CARDINAL variable. The value of the expression must always be positive if an error is not to occur. In the second statement, an array element is copied. Assignment of entire record and array values is also possible, as illustrated by the third statement. The last statement assigns the character-string "a" to the (longer) string field of

41

the fourth element of the record array currently referenced by the pointer variable point. (A variable accessed via a pointer in this way is usually created by means of the memory-allocation procedure ALLOCATE <see **Standard Modules**, p.102>.)

The assignment symbol := is usually referred to as "becomes".

4.3 IF..THEN statement

The IF..THEN statement is useful in cases where a number of alternative actions are required, each action being dependent on a different condition and/or having a different priority. It has the following form:

```
>     IF     boolExpr  THEN  statement  { ; statement }
      { ELSIF boolExpr  THEN  statement  { ; statement } }
      [ ELSE              statement  { ; statement } ]  END
```

where each *boolExpr* is an expression which delivers a BOOLEAN result. If the expression after the IF symbol evaluates to *true*, the statement sequence immediately following is executed. If the expression evaluates to *false*, each expression associated with an ELSIF clause is evaluated in turn until one delivers *true*, whereupon the corresponding statement sequence is executed. If none of the expressions evaluates to *true* (or if there are no ELSIF clauses), the statements belonging to the ELSE clause are executed instead, if present. Thus, only one statement sequence at most is executed.

Three examples of IF..THEN statements are:

```
IF (height < 50) THEN low:= TRUE   END

IF error THEN
  WriteString("oops!")
ELSE
  WriteString("ok!")
END


IF (var1 = var2) THEN
  WriteString("-- both equal --")
ELSIF (var1 > var2) THEN
  var2:= var1; WriteString("-- 2nd. increased --")
ELSE
  var1:= var2; WriteString("-- 1st. increased --")
END
```

Execution efficiency is highest when the alternative clauses are placed in the same order as their probability of occurrence.

IF..THEN statements can be used inappropriately. For example, the correct but rather clumsy statement

```
IF (height < 50) THEN
   low:= TRUE
ELSE
   low:= FALSE
END
```

can be much more economically expressed by the simple BOOLEAN assignment

```
low:= (height < 50)
```

4.4 CASE statement

The CASE statement is normally used when a number of alternative actions are possible, all dependent on the result of a single expression. The CASE statement has the form

>   CASE *expression* OF *alternative* { | *alternative* }
>   [ELSE *statement* { ; *statement* }] END

where each *alternative* has the form

>   [*caseRange* { , *caseRange* } :
                       statement { ; *statement* }]

Each *caseRange* specifies the values of *expression* which cause the associated statement sequence to be selected, and has the form

       constExpression [.. *constExpression*]

A single value is specified by a single expression, and a range of values (inclusive) by two expressions. The second, if used, should have a value greater than the first. The case ranges of different alternatives should not overlap, since an ambiguity would arise. The type of *expression* and of all instances of *constExpression* must be compatible, and can be CARDINAL,

INTEGER, CHAR, any enumerated type or any subrange of these.

When a CASE statement is executed, the selection expression is evaluated, and the statement sequence associated with the appropriate case range is then executed. If the expression value falls outside all the given case ranges, the statement sequence of the ELSE clause is executed instead (if present).

For example, if outCh is a CHAR variable, and heightStatus is a variable of the enumerated type (belowPath,onPath,abovePath), CASE statements such as the following might be used:

```
CASE outCh OF
"a".."z" :
   Write(CAP(outCh)) |
"A".."Z" :
   Write(outCh)
ELSE
  WriteString("char.number ");
  WriteCard(ORD(outCh))
END

CASE heightStatus OF
  belowPath :on( loLight);off(midLight);off(hiLight)|
  onPath    :on(midLight);off( loLight);off(hiLight)|
  abovePath :on( hiLight);off(midLight);off(loLight)
END
```

The CASE statement should not be confused with the similar syntax used to define the structure of variant records <see **Variant field**, p.19>. However, a CASE statement is often used to select the appropriate variant field of a record variable. For example, if recVar is of type RealorInt defined by

```
TYPE
   RealorInt = RECORD
               CASE isReal: BOOLEAN OF
                  TRUE  : realField : REAL    |
                  FALSE : intField  : INTEGER
               END (*CASE*)
            END (*RECORD*)
```

(which does not involve a CASE statement), then the correct field can be accessed using a CASE statement such as

```
CASE recVar.isReal OF
  TRUE  : WriteReal(recVar.realField,12) |
  FALSE : WriteInt (recVar.intField,8)
END (*CASE*)
```

44

4.5 FOR..DO statement

The FOR..DO statement is most useful when a particular statement sequence has to be repeated a fixed number of times, where the number is known beforehand. The FOR..DO statement has the form:

>   FOR *varIdent* := *expression* TO *expression*
>   [BY *constExpression*]
>   DO *statement* { ; *statement* } END

The identifier *varIdent* is the name of an existing variable (known as the *control variable*). This is set initially to the value of the first expression, then incremented repeatedly by the amount given by *constExpression* so long as its value remains within the range (inclusive) given by the first two expressions. (The expressions are evaluated once only, before the control variable is set for the first time. If the optional BY-clause is omitted, all values within the given range are used.) The given statement sequence is executed for each setting of the control variable. If there are no values of the control variable within the given range, the statement sequence is not executed at all.

A number of restrictions must be observed. The type of each limit expression must be compatible with that of the control variable. [There is some doubt as to which types are allowed, but certainly INTEGER and CARDINAL are valid. With many implementations, enumerated types, CHAR and any subrange of these types are also accepted.] The type of *constExpression* must be CARDINAL or INTEGER. The control variable can be any declared variable whose scope includes the FOR..DO statement and which belongs to the same module (ie. it cannot be a record field, an array element, a dereferenced pointer, a formal procedure parameter or an imported variable). **Neither the control variable nor any variable used in a limit expression should be changed by the statement sequence.** The value of the control variable at the end of the FOR..DO statement is undefined.

For example, assuming that limit is a CARDINAL constant or variable, pos and count are CARDINAL variables, and charArray is a character array, then FOR..DO statements such as the following two are valid:

```
FOR pos := 99 TO 0 BY -1 DO
   Write(charArray[pos]);
   charArray[pos]:= 0C
END

FOR count := 1 TO limit DO exp2:= exp2*2 END
```

4.6 WHILE..DO statement

This is used in situations where a statement sequence is to be repeated until a particular condition is fulfilled, the statements not being executed at all if the condition is met at the outset. It has the form

> WHILE *boolExpr* DO *statement* { ; *statement* } END

where *boolExpr* is a BOOLEAN expression (known as the *control expression*); the statement sequence is executed after the expression is evaluated, provided the result is *true*. This action is repeated until the expression returns *false*. (Normally, one or more variables used in the control expression are modified by the statement sequence so that termination does eventually occur.) The values of all variables used in a WHILE..DO statement remain valid after it has ended.

Examples of two WHILE..DO statements are:

```
WHILE (charArray[pos] # "!") DO pos:= pos+1   END

WHILE var1 < var2 DO
   var1 := var1 * 2;
   var2 := var2 DIV 2;
   count:= count + 1
END
```

4.7 REPEAT..UNTIL statement

This is used in situations where a statement sequence is to be repeated until a particular condition is fulfilled, the statements always being executed at least once. It has the form:

> REPEAT *statement* { ; *statement* } UNTIL *boolExpr*

where *boolExpr* is a BOOLEAN expression (the control expression).

46

The statement sequence is first executed and then the control expression is evaluated. This action is repeated so long as the expression returns the result *false*. (Normally, one or more variables used in the control expression are modified by the statement sequence so that termination does eventually occur.) The values of all variables used in a REPEAT..UNTIL statement remain valid after it has ended.

Two examples of REPEAT..UNTIL statements are:

```
REPEAT Read(ch) UNTIL (ch = EOL)

REPEAT
  search("Smith",name[index],done);
  index:= index+1
UNTIL done
```

In the second case, the BOOLEAN variable done is presumably set to *true* by the procedure search when the name "Smith" is found.

4.8 LOOP and EXIT statements

The LOOP statement is the most general repetition construct; it (potentially) repeats a given statement sequence forever. It has the form:

> LOOP *statement* { ; *statement* } END

The statement sequence is repeated indefinitely unless one of the statements causes the repetition to stop. For example, calling the standard procedure HALT will cause the entire program to terminate, while a RETURN statement will cause the currently-executing procedure to terminate. However, the most common way of ending a LOOP statement is by means of an EXIT statement. This has the form:

> EXIT

When an EXIT statement is executed, the innermost enclosing LOOP statement is terminated immediately, and execution continues with the statement following the LOOP statement. EXIT statements are normally placed within conditional

47

statements that control loop termination, ie. with the following general structure:

```
LOOP
    IF ( control expression ) THEN EXIT END
    ..
    ...additional statements ...
    ..
END (*LOOP*)
```

If no other EXIT statements are present, a loop of the above form has an effect similar to WHILE..DO. If the IF..THEN statement is placed at the end instead, the loop has the same effect as REPEAT..UNTIL. More general LOOP/EXIT combinations can be used to provide more complex actions such as loops which terminate in the middle of the statement sequence. For example, if count is a control variable of type (0..max), code with the general structure

```
count:= 0;
LOOP
    ..
    ... statements which use count ...
    ..
    IF (count >= max) THEN EXIT END;
    count:= count + 1
END (*LOOP*)
```

gives a loop where the termination condition also ensures that the control variable never exceeds its allowed range.

4.9 Procedure calls

Procedures (whether defined by procedure declarations or stored as values in procedure variables) are made to execute by giving the name of the procedure or procedure variable. This is known as a *procedure call*, and can have one of the following two forms:

>   *procident* [(*expression* { , *expression* })]

>   *varident* { *selector* } [(*expression* { , *expression* })]

48

The first form is used if the procedure is directly defined by a procedure declaration; *procIdent* is the procedure name, and can be a qualified identifier if required. The second form is used if the procedure is a procedure value; *varIdent* is a variable name which, followed by any suitable sequence of record field selectors, array element selectors and pointer dereferences, indicates the procedure variable (or procedure component of a variable) which holds the value. The variable name can be a qualified identifier.

The optional expressions within the round brackets, known as *actual parameters*, provide values and/or variables for use by the procedure when it executes. The actual parameters must match in both type and number with the formal parameters defined for the procedure <see **Procedures**, p.53>. Where the formal parameter is a VAR parameter, the equivalent actual parameter must be a variable (or a component of a variable), since the actual parameter can be modified by the procedure call. All expressions appearing as actual parameters are evaluated before the procedure begins.

If the procedure is a proper procedure (ie. one which does not return a value), the procedure call is a statement in its own right. Some examples of proper procedure calls are:

```
WriteString("hello!")    (* outputs a string value. *)

WriteLn                  (* takes no parameters.     *)

InOut.WriteLn            (* same as above, but uses *)
                         (* a qualified identifier. *)

Read(char)               (* a single-character is    *)
                         (* returned in <char>.       *)

Read(charArray[5])       (* the 5th. array element   *)
                         (* is set to the character *)
                         (* value which is read.      *)

procPtrArray[index]^     (* element of an array of   *)
                         (* pointers to procedures. *)
```

On the other hand, a value-returning procedure returns a result, and is therefore called as (part of) an expression within a statement rather than as a statement in its own right. The type of the expression in which the procedure call appears must

49

be compatible with the type of the returned value as given by the relevant procedure definition. Note that parameter brackets are obligatory in a value-returning procedure call, even if the procedure possesses no parameters (in which case the brackets will be empty).

Assuming procedure done returns a BOOLEAN value, procedure when (from module Timer) returns a CARDINAL value, and variable windowStruct is of type

```
RECORD
    ioProcs: POINTER TO ARRAY [indexType] OF POINTER TO
             RECORD
                 ...
             getChar : PROCEDURE (): CHAR
                 ...
             END; (*RECORD*)
    ...
END (*RECORD*)
```

then statements containing value-returning procedure calls such as the following are valid:

```
IF done() THEN EXIT END

time:= 2*Timer.when(input3,high) + 9

RETURN windowStruct.ioProcs^[index]^.getChar()
```

Parameter brackets are necessary in order that assignment of an **expression value** (where brackets are used and a value-returning procedure call is made) can be distinguished from assignment of a **procedure value** (where brackets are omitted and no procedure call is made). For example, if proc1 and proc2 are both variables of the procedure type PROCEDURE (): BOOLEAN, and bool is a BOOLEAN variable, then with

```
bool := proc1();
proc2:= proc1
```

the first statement is an assignment of a BOOLEAN value, obtained by executing the procedure value held in proc1, while the second is an assignment of a procedure value, namely that of proc1. The second statement involves no procedure execution.

50

4.10 RETURN statement

This statement terminates the procedure or module which executes it. Optionally, it also provides the return value needed for value-returning procedures. It has the form

> RETURN [*expression*]

where *expression*, if present, must be assignment-compatible with the return type of the procedure which contains the statement <see **Procedures**, p.53>. A procedure or module may contain any number of RETURN statements. A value-returning procedure must **always** terminate via a RETURN statement so that a return value is provided. A module or proper procedure need not, in which case the module or procedure terminates after the last statement in its statement sequence is executed.

Some examples of RETURN statements are:

```
RETURN TRUE                  (* BOOLEAN result *)

RETURN                       (* no result     *)

RETURN ptArray[index+offset] (* pointer result *)
```

4.11 WITH..DO statement

This evaluates a *record selection expression* so that it need not be repeated again within a given region of code. The form of this statement is:

> WITH *varIdent* { *selector* }
>   DO *statement* { ; *statement* } END

The record selection expression following the WITH symbol indicates the required record variable or record component of a variable <see **Record type**, p.18>. It consists of a variable name followed by any suitable sequence of record field selectors, array element selectors and pointer dereferences. The variable name can be a qualified identifier. If any expression evaluation is necessary, it is done once before the statements following the DO symbol are executed. All occurrences of the record selection expression within the statement sequence which otherwise would be necessary can be omitted; the record field names alone are now sufficient to identify the various fields.

For example, with the variable mySchool of type School defined by the following declaration:

```
TYPE
   String   = ARRAY [0..30] OF CHAR;
   Age      = [0..120];
   Child    = RECORD
                 firstName  : String
                 secondName : String;
                 age        : Age
              END; (*RECORD*);
   Class    = ARRAY [1..35] OF Child;
   Classes  = ARRAY [1..12] OF Class;
   School   = POINTER TO Classes;
```

then a statement sequence such as

```
WriteString(mySchool^[class][pupil].firstName);
WriteString(mySchool^[class][pupil].secondName);
WriteString(mySchool^[class][pupil].age);
mySchool^[class][pupil].age:=
                  mySchool^[class][pupil].age+1
```

can be condensed to the much simpler equivalent

```
WITH mySchool^[class][pupil] DO
   WriteString(firstName);
   WriteString(secondName);
   WriteString(age);
   age:= age+1
END
```

One restriction must be observed: none of the statements in the statement sequence should attempt to alter the identity of the record which is currently selected. However, this does not preclude a different record being selected each time the WITH..DO statement is executed. The following code fragment illustrates the difference:

```
index:= index+1;   (* allowed here *)
...

WITH recordArray[index] DO

   ...
   index:= index+1; (* ! not allowed here ! *)

   ...
END (*WITH*)
```

52

5 Procedures

5.1 General

The procedure is an important construct, because it allows a (typically complex) statement sequence to be abstracted into a single name. This avoids unnecessary repetition of code and makes code easier to write and understand. Procedures, in conjunction with types, are the means by which global modules provide facilities to other modules <see **Global modules**, p.61>.

The form of a procedure declaration is:

> PROCEDURE *ident* [([*paramDef* { ; *paramDef* }])
>   [: *typeIdent*]] ;
>   { *declaration* ; }
>   BEGIN *statement* { ; *statement* } END *ident* ;

where *ident* is the identifier which specifies the procedure name. (Note that it is given twice, at the beginning and also at the end.) Each *paramDef* defines one or more parameter variables (known as *formal parameters*) of a given type <see the next section>.

If present, the type identifier *typeIdent* indicates that the procedure returns a value of the given type, which can be any type other than a set, record, array or procedure type. The type identifier can be qualified. This kind of procedure is known as a *value-returning procedure*, and is always called by means of an expression of the appropriate type. The parameter brackets are obligatory in the declaration of such a procedure; they are empty if the procedure has no parameters. A procedure which does not return a value is known as a *proper procedure*, and is always called by means of a statement <see **Procedure calls**, p.48>.

The optional *declaration* allows the declaration of identifiers for local use within the procedure <see **Declarations**, p.32>.

The procedure statement sequence is enclosed by the BEGIN and END symbols.

53

5.2 Procedure parameters

It is often useful to be able to pass values to and from the procedure when it is called. This is achieved by defining *formal parameters*. A formal parameter is effectively a special local variable which, during a particular procedure call, is associated with a given external variable or value (known as the *actual parameter*). Otherwise, a formal parameter is the same as any other local variable, except that it cannot be the control variable of a FOR..DO statement.

The format of the formal parameter definition *paramDef* is:

>   [VAR] *ident* (, *ident*) : [ARRAY OF] *typeIdent*

Each *ident* specifies the name of a formal parameter, while *typeIdent* is an identifier which specifies the type of all the formal parameters in the list. The type identifier can be a qualified identifier.

The kind of association which is made between an actual and a formal parameter depends on which of the two available parameter-passing methods is chosen. If the reserved word VAR is omitted, the parameters in the list are *value parameters*, and the method is known as *pass-by-value*. In this case, the values of the actual parameters are directly copied to the corresponding formal parameters. (This can be somewhat inefficient with substantial data items such as large arrays). The formal parameters can be modified within the procedure, but any changes are not communicated back to the actual parameters. An actual parameter in this case must be assignment-compatible with the corresponding formal parameter.

On the other hand, if VAR is included, the formal parameters are *variable parameters*, and the method is known as *pass-by-reference*. In this case, the corresponding formal and actual parameters effectively become identical for the duration of the procedure call. Any assignment made to a formal parameter therefore also occurs to the corresponding actual parameter, and remains in effect after the end of the procedure call. Since actual parameters can be changed, they must be variables (or components of variables), and they must be type-compatible with the corresponding formal parameters.

Value parameters are normally used for "input only" data,

since actual parameters are then safe from being altered by the procedure call. Variable parameters are used if data must be passed back from the procedure. (A value-returning procedure can also be used to do this, but only if the data consists of a single unstructured value.) Variable parameters are the only means by which data can be passed in both directions. (With variable parameters, typically the only value copied is the address of the actual parameter, so variable parameters are usually more efficient than value parameters for large data items, and are therefore also sometimes used for "input-only" data. However, the actual parameters are then vulnerable to any changes made by the procedure, and must always be variables rather than general expressions.)

To illustrate, the following declaration defines a procedure which has a single **value** parameter:

```
PROCEDURE negate(par : INTEGER);

BEGIN
  par:= -par
END negate;
```

When the following code fragment is executed (where intVar is an INTEGER variable)

```
intVar:= 10;
negate(intVar);
WriteInt(intVar,2)
```

the value *10* is written out, because the actual parameter intVar is not affected when the formal parameter par is changed by the procedure. However, if the formal parameter is a **variable** parameter, ie. if the procedure declaration is instead

```
PROCEDURE negate(VAR par : INTEGER);

BEGIN
  par := -par
END negate;
```

then the value written out when the same code fragment is executed is now *-10*, because the change made to the formal parameter par is now also made to the actual parameter intVar.

5.3 Open-array parameters

Since the index range and type are part of an array type definition, array actual parameters must be of fixed size and index type. This restriction can sometimes be rather severe. For example, a procedure which accepts arrays of only one size is often very inconvenient for general-purpose use.

Open-array parameters are provided to lessen such difficulties. If the phrase ARRAY OF is included in a formal parameter definition, the parameter is an open-array parameter, and an array used as the corresponding actual parameter is then less rigidly constrained in respect of index type and size. Inside the procedure the index type is mapped to the subrange of CARDINAL [0..(n-1)], where n is the number of elements in the actual array. The base types of the formal and actual parameters, however, must still be type-compatible. For example, if the formal parameter is ARRAY OF BOOLEAN, an actual parameter of type ARRAY [1001..1006] OF BOOLEAN is mapped internally to the type ARRAY [0..5] OF BOOLEAN. If the formal parameter is a value parameter of type ARRAY OF CHAR, any character-string literal can be used as an actual parameter; eg. the actual parameter "abcd" is mapped to the type ARRAY [0..3] OF CHAR.

The upper index limit of any array actual parameter can be obtained by calling the standard procedure HIGH <see **Value-returning procedures**, p.92>. For example, Figure 5.1 shows a simple procedure which finds the average of all elements of any array of REAL values.

```
PROCEDURE average(values: ARRAY OF REAL) : REAL;

    VAR
       index, number : CARDINAL;
       sum           : REAL;

    BEGIN
       sum:= 0.0;
       number:= HIGH(values);
       FOR index:= 0 TO number DO
          sum:= sum+values[index];
       END; (*FOR*)

       RETURN sum/FLOAT(number+1)
    END average
```

Figure 5.1: Using an open array parameter

56

Because an open-array parameter has no defined size, it cannot be accessed as a whole, unlike other array variables (including normal array parameters). It must always be accessed element-by-element. However, it can be used as the actual parameter of another procedure, provided the corresponding formal parameter is also defined to be an open array.

5.4 Recursion

Since the scope of a procedure name includes the procedure's own statement sequence, a procedure is able to call itself. Such an action is known as *recursion*. In practice, the amount of recursion which can occur is limited, since an infinite recursion would never terminate [or more likely, would eventually fail]. A recursive procedure call is therefore usually placed inside an IF..THEN or CASE statement which at some appropriate point prevents the recursion from continuing. The value-returning procedure shown in Figure 5.2 is a typical example.

Recursion is particularly useful when an algorithm is best expressed in terms of itself. However, it should be used with care; each level of recursion consumes time and memory, so a very deep recursion is usually slow and can even fail for lack of space. Iteration (using statements such as WHILE..DO) often provides a more efficient if not always more convenient alternative <see **Statements**, p.40>.

```
PROCEDURE factorial(para: CARDINAL): CARDINAL;

(* This calculates the factorial function. *)

BEGIN
  IF (para > 1) THEN
    RETURN para * factorial(para-1)
  ELSE
    RETURN 1
  END (*IF*)
END factorial;
```

Figure 5.2: Recursive procedure call

5.5 Procedure local variables

A variable declared within a procedure is created when the procedure is called, exists for the duration of the procedure call, and is deleted when the procedure ends. Its initial value is undefined.

In the example of Figure 5.3, shareCh can be used to share data between procedures innerA and innerB because its lifetime is that of procedure outer. However, shareCh is also accessible to other procedures declared in outer (such as innerC) and also to outer itself <see **Scope of definitions**, p.38>. More exclusive sharing of a variable among procedures can be achieved by using a local module to limit the scope of the variable without affecting its lifetime. The variable can also be given an initial value if required <see **Module local variables**, p.74>.

```
PROCEDURE outer;


    VAR shareCh : CHAR;


    PROCEDURE innerA;
    BEGIN (*innerA*)
       (* <shareCh> is accessible here. *)
    END innerA;


    PROCEDURE innerB;
    BEGIN (*innerB*)
       (* <shareCh> is accessible here.*)
    END innerB;


    PROCEDURE innerC;
    BEGIN (*innerC*)
       (* <shareCh> is also accessible here. *)
    END innerC;


 BEGIN (*outer*)
    (* <shareCh> is also accessible here.*)
 END outer;
```

Figure 5.3: Sharing of a procedure local variable

6 Modules

6.1 General

The module is the main feature which distinguishes Modula from most other widely-used programming languages. It is a valuable aid in the creation of substantial software systems, since it enables a program to be constructed as a collection of mutually-supporting components (in the form of modules) rather than as a monolithic whole. For reliability and ease of construction, each module can be made as independent of the others as possible, and each is typically saved in a separate file. (In larger projects, a number of programmers will probably be involved at any given time, with everyone working on their own group of modules.) Nevertheless, when a facility provided by one module is used by any other, the full cross-checking capabilities of the language ensure that such usage is syntactically correct.

In many cases, the facilities provided by a module will be quite general-purpose, and will be reused by several programs. Modules which support widely-used tasks (eg. file-handling) may well accompany the compiler <see **Standard Modules**, p.94> or be available from other software sources. This provides additional saving of effort.

There are three different kinds of module. *Program modules* are modules which act as stand-alone programs. *Global modules* are modules which provide facilities used by other modules, rather than being executed directly. (The facilities typically take the form of a number of type and procedure definitions.) Both of these kinds of module form self-contained units. The third kind of module, the *local module*, does not exist on its own, but instead is embedded within a procedure or another module. It defines a region of code which can be isolated from the surrounding code in a highly-controlled way. This can bring improved software reliability.

Any of the above kinds of module can also be a *monitor*, which has special properties concerned with the protection of shared data in concurrent-programming environments.

6.2 Program modules

A program module is the kind which is used to create a normal executable program. It has the form:

> MODULE ident [[constExpression]];
> { importClause }
> { declaration }
> [BEGIN statement { ; statement }] END ident .

The identifier *ident* defines the program name; note that it is given both at the beginning and at the end. If *constExpression* within square brackets appears, the module is a monitor <see **Monitors**, p.72>. Each *declaration* is a normal declaration which defines identifiers that are local to the program <see **Declarations**, p.32>.

Each *importClause* specifies identifiers which are defined by other (ie. global) modules. It has the form:

> [FROM ident] IMPORT ident { , ident } ;

If the FROM part is omitted, all identifiers following the IMPORT symbol must be the names of global modules. Any identifier exported from a given module can then be used within the program module by qualifying it with the parent module name. For example, if the module InOut is imported using the import clause

    IMPORT InOut;

then procedures exported from InOut, eg. WriteString, can be called by statements such as

    InOut.WriteString("<- this uses a qualified name")

This kind of importation is most convenient when the same identifier is imported from more than one global module, since the presence of the (distinct) qualifiers prevents any name clashes occurring.

60

The second kind of importation applies when the FROM part is included in the import clause. In this case the identifier which follows the FROM symbol must be the name of a global module, and all identifiers in the following list must be ones exported by that module. These identifiers do not need to be qualified. Thus, if WriteString is imported explicitly with

```
FROM InOut IMPORT WriteString;
```

then the procedure call can be shortened to

```
WriteString("<- this uses an unqualified name")
```

This method is usually the most convenient way of importing an identifier, provided the identifier does not clash with the same one re-declared locally or imported from another global module.

Import of an enumerated type or a record type also implicitly imports the corresponding enumerated values and record field names. This sometimes causes name-clash errors which are hard to trace, because the offending identifiers do not themselves appear in any import or export clause. It is therefore best if such names are chosen to be unique in all circumstances <see **Enumerated type**, p.14>.

The statement sequence bracketed by the BEGIN and END symbols specifies the sequence of actions which the program performs when it is executed <see **Statements**, p.40>. Although the statement sequence is in principle optional, a program without one would be useless.

6.3 Global modules

A non-trivial Modula program typically consists of more than just a program module; it usually uses several global modules, each one performing some coherent part of the overall activity. Such modular construction brings a number of benefits. It minimises software complexity, and hence makes programs easier to understand and modify, thereby enhancing program reliability. It reduces overall compilation time, since only modules which have been modified need be recompiled, not the entire program. It allows general-purpose software packages to be produced whose facilities (types, procedures, etc.) are

61

available to any module which requires them. The full cross-checking capabilities of the language are maintained across all module boundaries.

Each global module is formed from two separate parts. The *definition module* specifies all publicly-available identifiers and their their public properties. The *implementation module* defines any private properties of public identifiers and also all purely-local identifiers. The public identifiers can be accessed by any other module via suitable IMPORT clauses; when such a client module is compiled, the definition module is read by the compiler so that it can check that all uses of public identifiers are consistent with their definitions. The definition module is also the only part which need be read by a programmer who is using the global module, since all public information about the global module is held there. For both these purposes, the implementation module is irrelevant, since it contains only private information (and in fact need not even exist).

Conversely, an implementation module can be altered (or totally replaced) as often as required without having any impact whatever on the coding of other modules, so long as it remains consistent with its definition module.

This separation of function between the two parts of a global module enables programs to be written, compiled and syntax-checked on the basis of agreed facilities (the definition parts) while still giving programmers maximum freedom concerning their implementation (the implementation parts).

The form of a definition module is:

>   DEFINITION MODULE *ident* ;
>   { *importClause* }
>   { *publicDecl* }
>   END *ident* .

As with other kinds of module, the identifier *ident* defines the module name, and *importClause* specifies imported identifiers. Each *publicDecl* defines identifiers exported by the module. It can consist of a normal TYPE, CONST or VAR declaration <see **Declarations**, p.32>. In the case of a normal type declaration, all details of the type (enumerated values, record field names, array index types and sizes, etc.) are automatically exported along with the type name. In the case of a variable declaration, the variable is accessible to any module which imports its name. Its lifetime is that of the importing module. (However, such variables do not provide very secure data sharing, and better methods are available <see **Monitors**, p.72>.)

There are two additional forms of *publicDecl*, one for types and the other for procedures. A public type declaration can be less complete than a normal type declaration, and has the general form:

> TYPE (*ident* [= *typeDesc*] ;)

Each *ident* specifies a type name. When the optional *typeDesc* (present in a normal type declaration) is omitted, the only externally-visible detail of the type is its name. This is known as *opaque export*. Such a type must be fully defined by a normal type declaration in the implementation module, and must be a pointer type.

Because values of an opaquely-exported type are private, they can only be created and modified by the parent global module; any facilities based on an opaquely-exported type must therefore be provided by a suitable group of (public) procedures belonging to the same module. This technique of information-hiding makes it possible to create high-level types which are widely accessible but nevertheless have values whose integrity is guaranteed.

The only operations directly available on opaquely-exported types are the equality relational operators (=, # and <>) and assignment. Note that an opaquely-exported type must be a pointer type, and the operations apply to the pointer, not to the variable referenced by it. Assignment therefore provides value-sharing rather than value-copying; the pointer value itself is assigned, not the value of the variable referenced by it. Likewise, the relational operators test for value-sharing rather than value-equality; it is the pointers that are compared, not the variables referenced by them.

The form of *publicDef* for a procedure is:

> PROCEDURE *ident* [([*paramDef* (; *paramDef*)])
>   [: *typeIdent*]] ;

63

```
DEFINITION MODULE IntStack;

(* This module provides Integer Stacks. *)


   TYPE
     IStack;
     Result  = (success,underflow,overflow);


   PROCEDURE clear(VAR stack : IStack);

   (* This makes an empty stack. It must be the *)
   (* first procedure used with each new stack. *)


   PROCEDURE push(value    : INTEGER;
                  VAR stack  : IStack;
                  VAR result : Result);

   (* This adds a value to the stack. *)


   PROCEDURE pop(VAR stack   : IStack;
                 VAR value   : INTEGER;
                 VAR result  : Result);

   (* This fetches a value from the stack. *)


   PROCEDURE size(stack     : IStack): CARDINAL;

   (* This gives the current size of the stack. *)

END IntStack.
```

Figure 6.1: Integer-stack definition module

This is identical to the header part of a normal procedure declaration <see **Procedure declarations**, p.35>. A full definition of the procedure must be provided by a normal procedure declaration in the implementation module.

As an example, Figure 6.1 shows the definition part of a global module which might be used to provide integer stacks. The values of the enumeration type Result are public, whereas those of type IStack are private, because the latter type is opaquely exported. The procedures push, pop, etc. provide typical stack operations. The names of the formal parameters used in the definition module are not important, and need not be the same as their equivalents in the implementation module, but they must be given nevertheless.

[Older implementations may require that all identifiers which are to be exported are indicated by a qualified export clause in exactly the same way as is done for a local module <see **Local modules**, p.69>.]

Facilities exported by a definition module are only visible (whether to the implementation module or to other modules) after the definition module has been compiled. Hence, although definition modules can import identifiers from other definition modules, such dependencies cannot be circular, since no module could then be compiled before any of the others.

Unlike other kinds of module, a definition module cannot have a statement sequence, and cannot indicate that it is a monitor; these properties are defined (as required) by the implementation module.

The form of an implementation module is:

>   IMPLEMENTATION MODULE *ident* [[*constExpression*]] ;
      { *importClause* }
      { *declaration* }
     [BEGIN *statement* { ; *statement* }] END *ident* .

This is the same as that of a program module except for the additional symbol IMPLEMENTATION <see **Program modules**, p.60>. Each *importClause* specifies identifiers imported from other global modules in the usual way. Since identifiers declared in a definition module are automatically visible in the corresponding implementation module, they are not imported explicitly by the implementation module. However, identifiers from other global modules which are required by both the definition and the implementation modules must be separately imported into each.

The declarations are normal type, constant, variable, procedure and module declarations <see **Declarations**, p.32>. They define all identifiers which are purely local to the implementation module, and also provide the full definitions of all procedures and opaquely-exported types which appear in public declarations in the corresponding definition module. Each such declaration must exactly match the public one, although the names of formal procedure parameters need not correspond (although it is good practice to ensure that they do). Complete declarations made in the definition module must not be repeated in the implementation module, since they are already valid there. Local identifiers of the implementation module are not visible elsewhere, not even in the corresponding definition module, and therefore cannot be imported by any other module.

An implementation module can possess a statement sequence, which is typically used to perform module initialisation. If a program or global module imports a global module, the imported module's statement sequence is automatically executed before that of the importing module. If a module imports a number of global modules, the statement sequences of the imported modules are executed in the same order of occurrence as given by the import clauses. [A circular dependency can in principle arise from imports to implementation modules; if so, the order of execution of the various statement sequences is not defined. Such a situation should therefore be avoided (it might also involve a more-obscure form of recursion).]

Continuing the example of the integer-stack module whose definition part was given in Figure 6.1, Figure 6.2 shows one possible version of a suitable implementation part. This can be replaced by any other version compatible with the same definition without any affect on code which uses the module's facilities. Of course, the exact functionality provided does depend on the implementation; with the version given, stack operations are relatively efficient, but the stacks have a fixed maximum size. Another version might avoid this restriction by taking a different approach, eg. by using a linked list.

```
IMPLEMENTATION MODULE IntStack;

(* This module provides Integer Stacks. *)
(*    -- fixed-size array version --    *)


   FROM SYSTEM IMPORT
     TSIZE;

   FROM Storage IMPORT
     ALLOCATE;


   CONST
     stackSize = 100;

   TYPE
     StackPos = [0..stackSize];
     IStack   = POINTER TO StackRec; (* full defn.*)
     StackRec = RECORD
                  top   : StackPos;
                  full  : BOOLEAN;
                  store : ARRAY StackPos OF INTEGER;
                END; (*RECORD*)


   PROCEDURE clear(VAR stack : IStack);

   (* This makes an empty stack. It must be the *)
   (* first procedure used with each new stack. *)

   BEGIN (*clear*)

      (* This obtains storage space and then  *)
      (* sets appropriate initial conditions. *)

      ALLOCATE(stack,TSIZE(StackRec));
      stack^.top:= 0;
      stack^.full:= FALSE
   END clear;


   PROCEDURE size(stack      : IStack): CARDINAL;

   (* This gives the current size of the stack. *)

   BEGIN (*size*)
     RETURN (stack^.top)
   END size;
```

Figure 6.2: Integer-stack implementation module

```
PROCEDURE push(value    : INTEGER;
               VAR stack  : IStack;
               VAR result : Result);

(* This adds a value to the stack. *)

BEGIN (*push*)
  IF (NOT stack^.full) THEN (* space available. *
    stack^.store[stack^.top]:= value;
    IF (stack^.top = stackSize) THEN
      stack^.full:= TRUE
    ELSE
      stack^.top:= stack^.top+1
    END; (*IF*)
    result:= succeed

  ELSE (* no more space. *)
    result:= overflow
  END; (*IF*)
END push;


PROCEDURE pop(VAR stack   : IStack;
              VAR value   : INTEGER;
              VAR result  : Result);

(* This fetches a value from the stack. *)

BEGIN (*pop*)
  IF (stack^.top > 0) THEN (* not at bottom. *)
    stack^.top:= stack^.top-1;
    value:= stack^.store[stack^.top];
    stack^.full:= FALSE;
    result:= succeed

  ELSE (* nothing in the stack. *)
    result:= underflow
  END; (*IF*)
END pop;

END IntStack.
```

Figure 6.2 (cont.): Integer-stack implementation module

6.4 Local modules

Unlike other modules, a local module is not self-standing, and is defined by a module declaration embedded within a procedure or within another module <see **Module declarations**, p.36>. A local module defines a region of code which is isolated in a highly-controlled way from the surrounding code. The visibility of all identifiers across the boundary is determined by a single explicit export clause (outwards) and/or various import clauses (inwards). The form of a local module is:

> MODULE *ident* [[*constExpression*]] ;
>   { *importClause* }
>   [*exportClause*]
>   { *declaration* }
>   [BEGIN *statement* { ; *statement* }] END *ident* ;

where (as with all other kinds of module) the two occurrences of *ident* define the name of the module. The presence of *constExpression* within square brackets indicates that the module is a monitor <see **Monitors**, p.72>. Each *declaration* is a normal declaration which defines identifiers local to the module <see **Declarations**, p.32>. Each *importClause* specifies identifiers which are imported from the surrounding scope, and has the same form as in other kinds of module, ie.

> [FROM *ident*] IMPORT *ident* { , *ident* } ;

If the FROM part is omitted, the given identifiers must be visible in the surrounding scope without qualification. If the FROM part is included, the identifier following the FROM symbol must be the name of a module which is visible in the surrounding scope, and all identifiers in the following list must be ones exported by that module.

The **single** export clause indicates those identifiers which are to be made visible in the surrounding scope. They must all be visible inside the local module, ie. they must be defined by local declarations or exported from local modules nested within the current one. An export clause has the form:

> EXPORT [QUALIFIED] *ident* { , *ident* } ;

```
MODULE local1;

    EXPORT ?QUALIFIED? local2;  .. qualified or not? ..


    MODULE local2;

    | EXPORT ?QUALIFIED? ident; .. qualified or not? ..

    |   .. <ident> is defined here ..

    END local2;


                    in this scope:

        <local2> export      <ident> accessed as:

            unqualified         ident
            qualified           local2.ident

END local1;


                    in this scope:

<local1> export      <local2> export      <ident> accessed as:

 unqualified          unqualified          ident
 unqualified          qualified            local2.ident
 qualified            unqualified          local1.ident
 qualified            qualified            local1.local2.ident
```

Figure 6.3: Exporting from local modules

70

If the QUALIFIED symbol is included, the identifiers are visible in the surrounding scope provided they are qualified by the name of the local module from which they are exported. If the QUALIFIED symbol is not given, the exported identifiers can be used in the surrounding scope without qualification. In this case, it is possible for name-clash errors to occur, since the same identifier can also be defined elsewhere and made visible in the same scope.

An export clause is sufficient to make the given identifiers visible in the surrounding scope; an additional import clause outside the module is not required. The following example illustrates export from local modules, in this case using type names:

```
MODULE local1;
  EXPORT Type1;
  TYPE Type1 = [0 .. 10];
END local1;


MODULE local2;
  EXPORT QUALIFIED Type2;
  TYPE Type2 = [-1 .. 1];
END local2;


VAR
  t1Var : Type1;          (* can be unqualified *)
  t2Var : local2.Type2; (* must be qualified   *)
```

[If an identifier exported from a local module is the name of an inner local module, identifiers exported from the inner module are visible both inside the local module and also in the outer code. The code fragment of Figure 6.3 illustrates the various possibilities for qualified and unqualified export from a local module.]

An identifier can be exported to any outer level or imported to any inner level provided it appears in all the relevant intermediate export or import clauses. Enumerated values and record field names automatically follow the parent type names.

A local module can possess a statement sequence. This is automatically executed before the statement sequence of the enclosing program or procedure is executed. If more than one local module is declared at the same level, their statement sequences are executed in the order in which the declarations occur. (Note that the statement sequence of a module which is local to a procedure will be executed each time the procedure is called.) The statement sequence is usually used to initialise the module's local variables <see **Module local variables**, p.74>.

6.5 Monitors

When the header of any module declaration includes a constant expression within square brackets, the module becomes a special one known as a *monitor*. This has some additional properties which are useful for concurrent-programming applications. A program is *fully concurrent* if several parts of it (known as *processes* or *tasks*) can actually or effectively be executing at the same time. In such a situation, data shared between processes can potentially be accessed by one process while still undergoing modification by another. A monitor makes it possible for data to be shared without such loss of integrity. Only one procedure of a monitor is allowed to be active at any one time, so if a process calls a monitor procedure while any of the procedures are already executing, the process is suspended until the currently-executing procedure ends. (If more than one process happens to be suspended when a monitor becomes "free" again, one of them is allowed to resume according to some unspecified selection scheme which is essentially random but which also ensures that no process is ever suspended indefinitely.) Data stored in variables which are local to the monitor (**not** global variables) can only be accessed via monitor procedures, and the monitor mechanism then ensures that the data always remains in a self-consistent state.

A program is *quasi-concurrent* if several parts of it (usually known as *coroutines*) can execute independently, but where only one part can be executing at a time, and a change of control from one part to another is achieved using an explicit transfer statement. Coroutines are supported in Modula by procedures NEWPROCESS and TRANSFER <see **Coroutines**, p.82>. When this is the only kind of concurrency provided, monitors are actually unnecessary, since one coroutine can never be preempted by another, and data will therefore never be encountered in an inconsistent state. Nevertheless, it is good practice to use a monitor anyway, since its presence at least clearly indicates

```
DEFINITION MODULE safeshare;


  PROCEDURE set(inChar       : CHAR): BOOLEAN;

  PROCEDURE get(VAR outChar : CHAR): BOOLEAN;

END safeshare.


IMPLEMENTATION MODULE safeshare [1];


  VAR
    shareCh : CHAR;        (* the shared variable.  *)
    new     : BOOLEAN;     (* its current state.    *)


  PROCEDURE set(inChar : CHAR): BOOLEAN;

  BEGIN
    IF (new) THEN          (* char. not yet taken:  *)
      RETURN FALSE         (*    fail is returned.   *)
    ELSE                   (* char. has been taken: *)
      shareCh:= inChar;    (*    new value is set,   *)
      new:=     TRUE;      (*    "new char" is set,  *)
      RETURN TRUE          (*    succeed is returned.*)
    END (*IF*)
  END set;


  PROCEDURE get(VAR outChar : CHAR): BOOLEAN;

  BEGIN
    IF (new) THEN          (* a new char. is ready: *)
      outChar:= shareCh;   (*    its value is taken, *)
      new:=     FALSE;     (*    "old char" is set,   *)
      RETURN TRUE          (*    succeed is returned.*)
    ELSE                   (* no new char. yet:       *)
      RETURN FALSE         (*    fail is returned.    *)
    END   (*IF*)
  END get;

BEGIN (*safeshare*)
  new:= FALSE;    (* "old char" is set initially. *)
END safeshare.
```

Figure 6.4: Example of a monitor

73

the function of the module.

Figure 6.4 gives an example of a fairly simple monitor which ensures that single characters can be safely passed from one process to another even in a fully-concurrent environment.

The constant expression within square brackets, whose presence indicates a monitor, must be compatible with type CARDINAL. It defines the *priority* of the monitor. In most cases, the actual value used is immaterial. However, there is one situation where the value is important. When an implementation is based on a processor with interrupt-driven peripherals (a common situation), a separate procedure, known as an *interrupt handler*, is used to process each kind of interrupt. The relevant interrupt handler is reactivated whenever a particular interrupt occurs <see **Coroutines**, p.82>. In this situation, the priority is used to ensure that interrupts can be selectively deferred to allow more important activities to be processed first. If the priority of the interrupt is higher than that of the procedure which is currently executing, the interrupt is processed immediately; if it is not, the interrupt is deferred until the current priority becomes low enough. The priority of a procedure is that of the module to which it belongs. Non-monitor modules have the lowest priority. A procedure used as an interrupt handler must be declared within a monitor, so that it has a well-defined priority. [This priority may possibly also have to correspond with a hardware-defined value.]

6.6 Module local variables

Variables declared within a global module have the same lifetime as those of the importing module (ie. program or global module), whether the variables are visible in the importing module or not. Consequently, all variables belonging to a global module have the same lifetime as the main program.

Variables declared within a local module have the same lifetime as those of the surrounding procedure or module, whether the variables are exported to the outside scope or not. A local module can therefore be used to provide exclusive data-sharing between procedures, as Figure 6.5 shows. The lifetime of shareCh is the same as that of the local variables of outer, but it is not accessible to outer or to any procedure declared within outer except those inside the local module. Note that the

74

names of procedures innerA and innerB must be exported from the local module so that they can be used outside it.

Because a local module's statement sequence is executed before that of the surrounding procedure or module, it can be used to initialise the module's local variables before the enclosing procedure or module begins. For example, with the module given in Figure 6.5, shareCh is initialised by the statement sequence of module protect. Each time outer is called, the variable shareCh is created anew and the module statement sequence is executed, thereby assigning an initial value to shareCh. This happens before the statement sequence of outer is executed, and hence before innerA or innerB can be called. The module statement sequence can be omitted if it is not needed.

```
PROCEDURE outer;

  MODULE protect;

    EXPORT innerA,innerB; (* exported to <outer> *)

    VAR shareCh : CHAR;


    PROCEDURE innerA;

    BEGIN (*innerA*)
      (* <shareCh> is accessible here. *)
    END innerA;


    PROCEDURE innerB;

    BEGIN (*innerB*)
      (* <shareCh> is accessible here.*)
    END innerB;


  BEGIN  (*protect*)
      shareCh:= 0C; (* this initialises <shareCh>.*)
  END protect;


  PROCEDURE innerC;

  BEGIN (*innerC*)
    (* <shareCh> is not accessible here. *)
  END innerC;


BEGIN (*outer*)
  (* <shareCh> is not accessible here.*)
END outer;
```

Figure 6.5: Protected sharing using a local module

7 Low-Level Facilities

7.1 General

In addition to its high-level features, Modula provides several facilities which make the language equally suitable for low-level applications such as systems programming, where greater freedom from constraint and/or a higher degree of control over the underlying system are needed. Some of these facilities are available directly as language constructs, while others (the majority) are exported from the module SYSTEM. Due to the special nature of its contents, the module SYSTEM is usually part of the compiler itself rather than existing as a separate global module, and hence it is often referred to as a *pseudo-module*. However, its facilities are imported in the same way as for other modules.

7.2 Type transfer

Although checking for type-compatibility in Modula is usually quite strict, it is possible to overcome this when necessary. This is achieved by means of a *type transfer*, which is an expression of the form

> *typeident (expression)*

The internal representation of the value given by *expression* is reinterpreted as a value of the type indicated by *typeident*. The latter can be the name of any type (including a user-defined type) which is visible in the current scope. **No processing or value conversion of any kind occurs**. The expression can be of any type, provided values of the type occupy the same amount of memory as those of *typeident*. [This demands detailed knowledge of the particular implementation being used. Code containing type transfers will not necessarily execute correctly on all implementations, since variables which are the same size in one implementation might not be in another.]

77

Examples of type-transfer expressions are:

REAL(5)   MyType(15)   CARDINAL(boolVar)

[Type transfer cannot in general be used to convert values of one type into equivalent values of another type. Even when the required effect is obtained, it might only apply to a restricted range of values; eg. with most implementations, conversion of an INTEGER value to a CARDINAL is possible, but it is only correct when the INTEGER value is positive.] Correct conversion between REAL and CARDINAL is possible using the standard procedures FLOAT and TRUNC <see **Value-returning procedures,** p.91 & p.93>. [Conversion between REAL and INTEGER is also usually possible by means of the procedures real and entier in module Mathlib <see **Standard Modules,** p.100>.]

7.3 Absolute-address variables

A variable declaration can specify the start address in memory of any variable, if required. (This is useful as a means of allowing access to hardware facilities such as i/o ports and i/o device status registers.) It is done by placing an address in square brackets after the variable name as follows:

>   *ident* [*constExpression*]

[The value given by *constExpression* must be integral, and must also be compatible with addresses in the implementation used].
For example, the declaration

    VAR
        kbPort[15],kbStatus[16],dataValue: CARDINAL;

creates three variables, two of which are located at the respective addresses 15 and 16, while the third is located at an address determined by the compiler in the normal way.
[If available, this facility should be used with great care. The addresses themselves are implementation-dependent, and may for example be byte or word addresses. Restrictions may be imposed on address values by the hardware; eg. byte addresses may have to be aligned to 2-byte or 4-byte boundaries.
The amount of memory used for a variable of any given type is

78

also implementation-dependent, so a declaration such as the above could result in the variables kbPort and kbStatus overlapping each other in memory (for example, if CARDINAL values occupy four bytes and the addresses are byte addresses).

This facility is not always available to general users. In a conventional multi-user system, for example, it would give any program direct access to operating system space and also to other programs' space. This could have potentially disastrous consequences if used by any program other than the operating system itself.]

In some cases, can be easier and safer to declare a variable in the usual way, then obtain its address afterwards using the procedure ADR <see **Memory-enquiry procedures**, p.81>.

7.4 Type BITSET

This is a special type defined as SET OF [0..(n-1)], where n is a small constant which is implementation-dependent [and is typically the word length of the processor or a small multiple of it]. It is a standard type, and the usual set operators and literal constants can be used <see **Set type**, p.16>. A set literal constant which has no name prefix (eg. {0,3}) is of type BITSET.

[This type is useful for setting and masking bits in registers; for example, if kbStatus is a variable which represents a device status register, then the assignment

        kbStatus:= {1,2,3}

will typically set the bits in positions 1, 2 and 3 to the '1' state and all others to the '0' state. The statement

        kbStatus:= kbStatus - {1,2,3}

will typically clear the bits in positions 1, 2 and 3 while leaving the others unchanged.]

7.5 Types WORD and ADDRESS

These two low-level types are usually provided by the pseudo-module SYSTEM. They support dynamic memory allocation and generic procedure calls. WORD is defined as representing an individually-accessible unit of memory. [The actual size of this

79

unit is implementation-dependent, and might be a byte, a 16-bit word or a 32-bit word. Some implementations do not adhere to this definition; for example, WORD is sometimes arranged to occupy the same amount of storage as CARDINAL or ADDRESS (typically 16 or 32 bits) even when the memory is byte-addressible. In such cases, the additional type BYTE may be provided by module SYSTEM to allow access to byte-size units.]

No WORD operations are provided (not even comparison), since WORD values are regarded as possessing no inherent interpretation. However, assignment and parameter-passing of WORD values are allowed, and type transfer enables the values to be converted into values of other types ‹see **Type transfer**, p.77›.

If a formal procedure parameter is of type WORD, the actual parameter may be of any type which occupies the same amount of memory. This makes it possible to create a *generic procedure*, ie. a procedure which accepts parameters of different types, provided they are all of single-word size. [The range of suitable types is implementation-dependent; it often includes CARDINAL, INTEGER, BITSET and pointer types. However, with a given implementation it might possibly not include any standard types at all.]

A formal parameter of type ARRAY OF WORD is compatible with an actual parameter of any size and type (including data structures such as arrays and records), thereby making possible unrestricted generic procedures. The actual size in memory of any particular parameter (or of its components, where relevant) can be found by means of the procedures SIZE and TSIZE ‹see below, p.81›.

The type ADDRESS is defined as being POINTER TO WORD, and is compatible with all pointer types and also with type CARDINAL; arithmetic operations are therefore possible using combinations of ADDRESS and CARDINAL values. [Unfortunately, not all implementations adhere strictly to this definition; for example, some make ADDRESS compatible with LONGCARD instead of CARDINAL. Also, the underlying hardware can impose restrictions on the values used; eg. byte addresses may have to be 2-byte (odd or even) or 4-byte aligned. A good knowledge of the implementation is therefore essential if such address manipulation is to succeed. Its greatest usefulness is for applications such as dynamic memory management.]

7.6 Memory-enquiry procedures

Three procedures (ADR, SIZE and TSIZE) are usually provided by SYSTEM to provide information about the allocation of memory to variables. These are particularly useful for supporting dynamic memory allocation, along with procedures such as ALLOCATE and DEALLOCATE from module Storage <see **Standard Modules,** p.102>, and are defined as follows:

ADR(*varIdent*)

This provides the address in memory of the variable *varIdent*, which can be of any type. The result is of type ADDRESS, and is the start address of the given variable in memory. The parameter must be a variable name, and cannot be a constant or an expression. The name used must be visible in the current scope. [Addresses are implementation-dependent, so a value produced by ADR cannot in general be assumed to be a byte, word or any other particular kind of address.]

For example, in the procedure call

```
writeToDisc(ADR(buffer),1024)
```

the first parameter of procedure writeToDisc is the start address of the variable buffer.

SIZE(*varIdent*)

This returns the size in words occupied by the variable given by *varIdent*. The result is of type CARDINAL. The variable used must be visible in the current scope. [Some implementations do not use word-size units, but other units such as bytes or multiple-words. For example, the following results might be obtained in some cases:

```
        SIZE(charVar)  ->      1
        SIZE(wordVar)  ->      4
        SIZE(cardVar)  ->      4          ]
```

TSIZE(*typeIdent*)

This returns the size in words occupied by variables of the type given by *typeIdent*. In the case of a variant record, the size is that of the largest possible variant. The type name used must be visible in the current scope. The result is of type CARDINAL.

[Some implementations do not use word-size units, but other units such as bytes or multiple-words. For example, the following results might possibly be obtained:

```
TSIZE(CHAR)       ->    1
TSIZE(WORD)       ->    4
TSIZE(CARDINAL)   ->    4         ]
```

[Some implementations provide SIZE as a standard procedure, not as a procedure exported from SYSTEM. In this case, SIZE may possibly accept the names of types as well as those of variables, and the return type of TSIZE is implementation-dependent. The continued need for TSIZE in such a situation is rather unclear!]

7.7 Coroutines

Quasi-concurrent programming in the form of coroutines is supported by module SYSTEM via procedures NEWPROCESS and TRANSFER. The first creates a coroutine from an existing procedure (without causing a transfer of control), while the second causes a transfer of control from the currently-executing coroutine to the given coroutine. The specification of NEWPROCESS is:

```
PROCEDURE NEWPROCESS(sourceProc      : PROC;
                     wkSpace          : ADDRESS;
                     wkSpaceSize      : CARDINAL;
                     VAR startCEPt    : ADDRESS)
```

The procedure used to form the coroutine is given by sourceProc, which can be either a declared procedure or a procedure variable. It must be parameterless (ie. of type PROC) and must be declared at the outermost scope level (ie. in the main program or in a global module). The initial point of execution of the coroutine is placed at the address returned in parameter startCEPt. [In older implementations this parameter is of type PROCESS, a type exported from SYSTEM.]

The parameters wkSpace and wkSpaceSize define the start address and size of the memory region which is used for storing the coroutine's local variables. [There is no simple means of determining the size of workspace required in any particular

82

case. In practice, it is often calculated as a fixed minimum value plus the combined size of all variables which are local to the coroutine procedure (in storage units, whatever they may be for the implementation used). If a formula for the required size is not given in the implementation documentation, the optimum value can usually be found by the following crude but effective method: a generous initial memory allocation should be made, then reduced progressively until the minimum size is found for which the program still executes without failing; a small margin can then be added to this minimum size for safety.]

Any number of coroutines can be created from the same original procedure by making repeated calls to NEWPROCESS; different variables for startCEPt and different memory areas for wkSpace should be used each time if the coroutines are all to exist concurrently.

Transfer of control from the currently-executing coroutine to another is done explicitly by calling procedure TRANSFER. This has the specification:

```
PROCEDURE TRANSFER(VAR saveCEPt, nextCEPt : ADDRESS)
```

[In older implementations, both parameters of TRANSFER are of type PROCESS.]

When this procedure is called, the current point of execution is saved in the first parameter. Control then transfers to the address given in the second parameter, and execution continues from there. (The second parameter is accepted before the first is saved, so the same variable can safely be used for both actual parameters, if required.) Execution can be made to resume from any previously-suspended address by calling TRANSFER again with that address as the second parameter.

In this way, any number of coroutines can exist concurrently. For each one there is a current point of execution, set initially by NEWPROCESS. A coroutine resumes execution when control is passed to it because its current execution point is given to TRANSFER, and is re-suspended (its current point of execution being saved again) when it in turn passes control to another coroutine via TRANSFER. The program terminates whenever the end of the currently-executing coroutine is reached, whether it is the main program or not.

It can be convenient to delegate the task of performing all transfers of control to a dedicated subsystem (known as a *scheduler*) instead of having calls to TRANSFER scattered throughout a program. One module which provides this function is Processes <see **Standard Modules**, p.103>.

Since input/output devices usually function independently of the processor, an additional facility is sometimes provided by SYSTEM to support this form of (true) concurrency. Typically, each time a value is available from an input device (such as a character typed on the keyboard), normal execution of the processor is suspended by an interrupt sent by the device, and the processor temporarily executes a process known as an *interrupt handler* or *device handler* which performs the actions needed to accept the value. When these are finished, the processor resumes its previous activity from the point at which it was interrupted. Likewise, when an output device (such as a printer) is ready to accept a new value, it sends an interrupt to activate its handler to produce the next value.

In Modula, each interrupt handler is created using NEWPROCESS and started by calling TRANSFER as described above. However, after the interrupt handler has completed its initial actions, it relinquishes control by calling the procedure IOTRANSFER, not TRANSFER as a normal coroutine would do. IOTRANSFER does more than transfer control; it also ensures that the interrupt handler is automatically resumed whenever an interrupt is sent by the associated device. Explicit transfers to the interrupt handler are not needed. So long as device activity is required, the interrupt handler continues to relinquish control by calling IOTRANSFER. When device activity is no longer required, a normal transfer of control using TRANSFER ensures that subsequent interrupts from the device will be ignored until the device handler is restarted.

The specification of IOTRANSFER is as follows:

```
PROCEDURE IOTRANSFER(VAR intHandlerCEPt,
                         mainCEPt        : ADDRESS;
                         intVector       : CARDINAL)
```

[In older implementations, the first two parameters are of type PROCESS.]

As with TRANSFER, the current point of execution (of the

84

interrupt handler in this case) is saved in `intHandlerCEPt` and a transfer is made to the address given by `mainCEPt`. (Initially `mainCEPt` is the point at which execution is suspended when the interrupt handler is started by an explicit call of TRANSFER. Subsequently it is the point at which execution is suspended when the interrupt handler automatically resumes because of an interrupt arriving from the associated device.)

The third parameter, `intVector`, specifies the actual interrupt source which will cause this interrupt handler to be resumed. [Its value is implementation-dependent, but usually is an address associated with a particular interrupt source which is read by the processor when an interrupt is received from that source; it might contain the address of the current execution point of the relevant interrupt handler, ie. of the variable `intHandlerCEPt`.]

In general, a number of interrupt handlers may be active, each supporting its own particular device. Interrupts can occur while any coroutine or interrupt handler is executing. In this situation, it is sometimes necessary to ensure that certain critical activities (eg. accessing shared variables or altering the contents of device control registers) can only be interrupted by events of even greater importance. Less-important interrupts must then be deferred until the current activities have been completed. For example, interrupts from fast devices are usually given priority over slow devices so that throughput is not slowed down unnecessarily. It is therefore obligatory for an interrupt-handler procedure to be declared within a monitor module; the priority of the interrupt handler is the same as that of the monitor <see **Monitors**, p.72>. An interrupt is deferred whenever the priority of its interrupt handler is less than or equal to the priority of the currently-executing procedure.

[Interrupt-handling is an activity which is at the heart of nearly all computer systems. Some implementations therefore do not make IOTRANSFER available for general use, since its misuse would severely disrupt the system. This is particularly true for multi-user systems. IOTRANSFER is generally confined to systems software and to programs which have to run without the support of an underlying operating system.]

Figures 7.1 and 7.2 give an example of a global module which uses TRANSFER and IOTRANSFER to provide interrupt-handling. The code is typical of that needed for memory-mapped devices, although the timer in this case is hypothetical (but realistic). The timer is accessed via two absolute-address variables, one for the timer's status register and the other for its time count. The position of these two variables in memory and the value of the device interrupt vector (timerIV) are hardware-dependent. In the code given, the timer is started automatically as part of the module initialisation sequence, but this is optional.

```
DEFINITION MODULE SysClock;

(* This supports a hardware system clock. *)

    TYPE
        Time : CARDINAL;

    PROCEDURE getTime (): Time;

    (* This gets the latest time (in seconds). *)

    PROCEDURE startClock;

    (* This starts the system clock. *)

    PROCEDURE stopClock;

    (* This stops the system clock.  *)

END SysClock.
```

Figure 7.1: An example interrupt-handler
(definition module)

```
IMPLEMENTATION MODULE SysClock[1];


FROM SYSTEM IMPORT
  ADDRESS,NEWPROCESS,TRANSFER,IOTRANSFER;

FROM Storage IMPORT
  ALLOCATE;


VAR
  time       : Time;     (* current time (secs).  *)
  running    : BOOLEAN;  (* the current state.    *)
  mainESP    : ADDRESS;  (* mainstream execution- *)
                         (* suspension point.     *)
  handESP    : ADDRESS;  (* handler execution-    *)
                         (* suspension point.     *)
  wkSpace    : ADDRESS;  (* its workspace address.*)

  (* The next two variables are respectively    *)
  (* the timer status and data registers. The   *)
  (* timer is enabled/disabled by setting the    *)
  (* 16th. bit of the status register to 1 or 0.*)
  (* Bits 0-5 set the interrupt interval(ticks).*)

  timSR[22] : BitSet; (* the status register.   *)
  timDR[23] : Time;   (* the data register.     *)


CONST
  intInterval = {0,1,2,3,4}; (* equals 63 ticks.*)
  timerIV     = 5;   (* timer interrupt vector. *)
  wkSize      = 100; (* handler workspace size. *)
  enableBit   = 16;  (* the timer enable bit.   *)


PROCEDURE getTime(): Time;

(* This gets the latest time. *)

BEGIN (*getTime*)
  RETURN time
END getTime;
```

Figure 7.2: An example interrupt-handler
(implementation module)

87

```
PROCEDURE startClock;  (* This starts the clock. *)

BEGIN (*startClock*)
  time:=  0;
  timDR:= 0; (* this resets the timer register. *)
  IF (NOT running) THEN
    running:= TRUE;

      (* The int. rate is set, the timer enabled, *)
      (* and the timer handler is started-up:     *)
      timSR:= intInterval+{enableBit};
      TRANSFER(mainESP,handESP)
  END (*IF*)
END startClock;


PROCEDURE stopClock;     (* This stops the clock   *)
                         (* at the next interrupt. *)
BEGIN (*stopClock*)
  running:= FALSE;
END stopClock;


PROCEDURE timerHandler;

(* This is the timer interrupt-handler proc. *)

BEGIN (*timerHandler*)

  WHILE (running) DO    (* read the time and wait  *)
    time:= timDR;       (* for the next interrupt: *)
    IOTRANSFER(handESP,mainESP,timerIV);
  END; (*WHILE*)

  timSR:= {};       (* stop the timer and resume  *)
  TRANSFER(handESP,mainESP); (* the mainstream. *)
END timerHandler;

BEGIN (*SysClock*)    (* module initialisation. *)

  (* This creates the timer interrupt handler: *)
  ALLOCATE(wkSpace,wkSize);
  NEWPROCESS(timerkHandler,wkSpace,wkSize,handESP);

  running:= FALSE; (* this sets the initial state. *)
  startClock;      (* <- optional automatic start. *)

END SysClock.
```

Figure 7.2 (cont.): An example interrupt-handler
(implementation module)

8 Standard Procedures

8.1 General

A number of procedures (known as *standard procedures*) are supplied as predefined identifiers, ie. they are used directly rather than being imported from any module. As with other procedures, there are two kinds: those which return a value (ie. value-returning procedures) and those which do not (ie. proper procedures). Unlike normal procedures, however, they have the special property that they can accept various numbers and types of parameter, and (in the case of value-returning procedures) can return values of more than one type. A standard procedure cannot be assigned to a procedure variable nor used as an actual parameter in a procedure call.

8.2 Proper procedures

The following proper procedures are available:

DEC(*varIdent*)
DEC(*varIdent,expression*)

This decrements the variable *varIdent* either by one step (if *expression* is omitted) or by the number of steps given by the expression, which must be of type INTEGER or CARDINAL. The type of the variable can be any enumerated type, INTEGER, CARDINAL, CHAR or any subrange of these. If the result would be outside the allowed range of values, it is undefined. For example,

```
DEC(boolVar)      (* before: true;  after: false  *)
DEC(charVar,2)    (* before: "c";   after: "a"    *)
DEC(intVar,10)    (* before: 19;    after: 9      *)
DEC(boolVar)      (* before: false  after: ????   *)
```

EXCL(*varIdent,expression*)

This removes the element given by *expression* from the given set variable *varIdent* if it is currently in the set. The type of *expression* must be the same as the base type of the set. For example (assuming `tripletVar` is of type `Triplet`),

```
  EXCL(tripletVar,1)    (* before: Triplet{0,1,2}   *)
                        (* after:  Triplet{0,2}     *)
   EXCL(tripletVar,0)   (* before: Triplet{2,4,6}   *)
                        (* before: Triplet{2,4,6}   *)
```

(In general the expression need not be a constant one, as used above. [Some older implementations, however, do impose this restriction.])

HALT

This stops the program. [In some implementations, it also causes an error message to be issued.]

INC(*varIdent*)
INC(*varIdent,expression*)

This is similar to DEC, but increments the variable rather than decrements it. For example,

```
   INC(boolVar)        (* before: false;  after: true   *)
   INC(charVar,5)      (* before: "a";    after: "f"    *)
   INC(intVar,10)      (* before: 19;     after: 29     *)
   INC(boolVar)        (* before: true    after: ????   *)
```

INCL(*varIdent,expression*)

This is similar to EXCL, but adds an element to the given set variable if it does not belong to the set already. The type of *expression* must be the same as the base type of the set. For example (assuming `tripletVar` is of type `Triplet`),

```
   INCL(tripletVar,2)   (* before: Triplet{0,1};     *)
                        (* after:  Triplet{0,1,2}    *)
   INCL(tripletVar,1)   (* before: Triplet{0,1,2,3}  *)
                        (* after:  Triplet{0,1,2,3}  *)
```

(In general the expression need not be a constant one, as used above. [Some older implementations, however, do impose this restriction.])

8.3 Value-returning procedures

The following value-returning procedures are available:

ABS(*expression*)

This calculates the absolute value of the given expression. The type of the result is the same as that of the expression, which can be any numerical type (eg. INTEGER or REAL). For example,

```
ABS (-55.0)   ->        55.0
ABS (-15)     ->        15
ABS (9)       ->        9
```

CAP(*expression*)

This converts the expression value (which must be of type CHAR) to upper case if it is a letter; if the value is not a letter, the result is undefined. For example,

```
CAP ("a")     ->        "A"
CAP ("A")     ->        "A"
CAP ("?")     ->        undefined
```

CHR(*expression*)

This converts the ordinal number given by *expression* into the equivalent character. It is equivalent to VAL(CHAR,*expression*). [The exact correspondence depends on the ordering of the character set used by the implementation; for example, with the ISO/ASCII set:

```
CHR (32)      ->        " "   (ie. space)
CHR (97)      ->        "a"
CHR (13)      ->        .cr.  (ie. carriage return) ]
```

FLOAT(*expression*)

This returns the value of type REAL which is equivalent to the CARDINAL (not INTEGER!) value given by *expression*. For example,

```
FLOAT (3)     ->        3.0
FLOAT (0)     ->        0.0
```

HIGH(*arrayIdent*)

This returns the index upper bound of the one-dimensional array variable *arrayIdent*. For example, if `arrayVar` is a variable of type `ARRAY [0..15] OF CHAR`, then

$$\text{HIGH(arrayVar)} \quad \rightarrow \quad 15$$

(This is often used in a procedure with an open-array parameter to obtain the size of the array provided as the actual parameter <see **Open-array parameters**, p.56>.)

MAX(*typeIdent*)
MIN(*typeIdent*)

These respectively provide the maximum and minimum values of the type given by *typeIdent*. The result type is the same as that of *typeIdent*. [This can be any enumerated type, `CARDINAL`, `INTEGER`, any subrange of these, and perhaps `REAL`. For example,

$$\text{MAX(CARDINAL)} \quad \rightarrow \quad 65535$$
$$\text{MIN(INTEGER)} \quad \rightarrow \quad -32768$$

The results are implementation-dependent. These procedures are sometimes not provided at all by older implementations.]

ODD(*expression*)

This returns the `BOOLEAN` result *true* when the value given by *expression* is odd and *false* when it is even. [The expression can be of type `CARDINAL`, `INTEGER` or any subrange of these.] For example,

$$\text{ODD(3)} \quad \rightarrow \quad \textit{true}$$
$$\text{ODD(8)} \quad \rightarrow \quad \textit{false}$$

ORD(*expression*)

This returns the ordinal number (as a `CARDINAL` value) of *expression*, whose type can be any enumerated type, `CARDINAL`, `INTEGER`, `CHAR` or any subrange of these. For example,

$$\text{ORD(FALSE)} \quad \rightarrow \quad 0$$
$$[\quad \text{ORD("a")} \quad \rightarrow \quad 97 \text{ (for the ISO/ASCII set) }]$$

TRUNC(*expression*)

This converts the REAL value given by *expression* into one of type CARDINAL (**not** INTEGER!) by truncating the real value to its integral part. For example,

```
TRUNC(3.14159)  ->      3
TRUNC(9.99999)  ->      9
```

VAL(*typeIdent,expression*)

This returns the value of the type given by *typeIdent* whose ordinal number is given by *expression*. The expression must be of CARDINAL type or a subrange of CARDINAL. The type given by *typeIdent* must be an enumerated type, CHAR, INTEGER, or CARDINAL, or a subrange of these. For example,

```
      VAL(BOOLEAN,0)  ->      false
[     VAL(CHAR,33)    ->      "!"  (for the ISO/ASCII set)  ]
```

[In some implementations, the procedure SIZE is also provided as a standard procedure, rather than being exported from module SYSTEM <see **Memory-enquiry procedures**, p.81>; if SIZE is a standard procedure, it usually accepts either a variable name or a type name, unlike the version exported from SYSTEM.]

[In implementations which provide the extended-precision types LONGCARD and LONGREAL <see **Type CARDINAL**, p.9 and **Type REAL**, p.12>, procedures TRUNCD and FLOATD are usually also available as standard procedures which convert between values of the two types (in a similar way to TRUNC and FLOAT).]

9 Standard Modules

9.1 General

A number of global modules are usually provided as part of a Modula implementation. [Currently none are standardised, so despite the term "standard module", in practice they can vary somewhat in name and content. However, if the facilities are not always identical, they are usually not too dissimilar. The descriptions given here can therefore serve as a general guide, even though they may differ in detail from those applying to any given implementation. It is possible that none of the modules described here are provided by an implementation; conversely (and more likely), many more modules may be provided than described here. Implementation documentation should therefore be consulted to determine exactly what facilities are available.] The modules described here are:

* Terminal   - simple terminal input/output

* InOut   - general file input/output

* RealInOut - additional real-number i/o

* MathLib   - some useful mathematical functions

* Storage   - dynamic memory allocation

* Processes - coroutine scheduling/synchronisation

In each case the module is described by presenting it in the form of a definition module.

DEFINITION MODULE Terminal;

(* This provides simple terminal input/output. *)

PROCEDURE Read(VAR inChar : CHAR);
(* This gets a character from the keyboard, *)
(* waiting if necessary for it to be entered. *)

PROCEDURE BusyRead(VAR inChar : CHAR);
(* This gets a character immediately; if no *)
(* key has been pressed, <null> is returned. *)

PROCEDURE ReadAgain;
(* This causes the next read to get the previous *)
(* character entered rather than the next one. *)
(*   --- (not always provided) ---   *)

PROCEDURE Write(outChar : CHAR);
(* This writes out a single character. *)

PROCEDURE WriteString(outStr : ARRAY OF CHAR);
(* This writes out a character string. *)

PROCEDURE WriteLn;
(* This begins a new line of output. *)

PROCEDURE ClearTerminal;
(* This clears the screen on a VDU terminal; *)
(*   --- (not always provided) ---   *)

END Terminal.

DEFINITION MODULE InOut;

(* This provides simple terminal & file input/output. *)

CONST
EOL = 15C;　　　　　(* This value depends on　*)
　　　　　　　　　　(* the implementation !　　*)

VAR
Done　　: BOOLEAN;　(* Operation result status. *)
termCh : CHAR　　　(* Termination character. *)

PROCEDURE OpenInput(defExt : ARRAY OF CHAR);
(* This causes subsequent input to be taken from *)
(* a file; a prompt is issued and the file name is *)
(* read from the terminal. If the name entered　　*)
(* ends with a period, the suffix defExt is added. *)
(* Done indicates success/fail of the operation.　*)

PROCEDURE CloseInput;
(* This causes subsequent input to be　*)
(* taken from the terminal again.　　　*)

PROCEDURE OpenOutput(defExt : ARRAY OF CHAR);
(* This causes subsequent output to be written to *)
(* a file; a prompt is issued and the file name is　*)
(* read from the terminal. If the name entered　　*)
(* ends with a period, the suffix defExt is added. *)
(* Done indicates success/fail of the operation.　*)

PROCEDURE CloseOutput;
(* This causes subsequent output to　*)
(* be written to the terminal again.　*)

PROCEDURE Read(VAR inChar : CHAR);
(* This gets a single character from the current *)
(* input source. If the source is a file, *Done* is *)
(* TRUE afterwards if there is more to be read. *)

PROCEDURE ReadString(VAR inString : ARRAY OF CHAR);
(* This gets a character string from the current *)
(* input source, terminated by a space or control *)
(* character. Leading spaces are ignored. *termCh* *)
(* contains the char. which terminated the string. *)

PROCEDURE ReadInt(VAR inInt : INTEGER);
(* This gets an INTEGER value from the current *)
(* input source. The syntax accepted is: *)
(*   { space } [+|-] digit { digit } *)
(* *Done* is set TRUE if a valid value was found. *)

PROCEDURE ReadCard(VAR inCard : CARDINAL);
(* This gets a CARDINAL value from the current *)
(* input source. The syntax accepted is: *)
(*   { space } digit { digit } *)
(* *Done* is set TRUE if a valid value was found. *)

```
PROCEDURE WriteLn;
(* This begins a new line of output. *)


PROCEDURE Write(outChar : CHAR);
(* This writes a character to the current output. *)


PROCEDURE WriteString(outStr : ARRAY OF CHAR);
(* This writes a string to the current output. *)


PROCEDURE WriteInt(outInt      : INTEGER;
                   fieldWidth   : CARDINAL);
(* This writes an INTEGER to the current output. *)
(* If the value fits within a field of the given  *)
(* width, it is right-justified in that field.     *)


PROCEDURE WriteCard(outCard    : CARDINAL;
                    fieldWidth : CARDINAL);
(* This writes a CARDINAL to the current output.*)
(* If the value fits within a field of the given  *)
(* width, it is right-justified in that field.     *)


PROCEDURE WriteOct(outCard     : CARDINAL;
                   fieldWidth  : CARDINAL);
(* As WriteCard, but using octal format. *)


PROCEDURE WriteHex(outCard     : CARDINAL;
                   fieldWidth  : CARDINAL);
(* As WriteCard, but using hexadecimal format. *)


END InOut.
```

DEFINITION MODULE RealInOut;

(* This provides input/output for real numbers. *)

VAR
    Done : BOOLEAN;   (* ! not the same variable   *)
                      (*   as that of module InOut ! *)

PROCEDURE ReadReal(VAR inReal : REAL);
(* This reads a REAL value from the current   *)
(* input source set by *InOut*. The syntax used is: *)
(* { space } [+|-] digit { digit } [. { digit }]   *)
(*   [E [+|-] digit { digit }] *)
(* *Done* is set TRUE if a valid value was found. *)

PROCEDURE WriteReal(outReal   : REAL ;
                     sigDigits : CARDINAL);
(* This writes a REAL value to the output currently *)
(* set by *InOut*, showing the given no. of sig. digits. *)

(* This module is sometimes subsumed in module *InOut*. *)

END RealInOut.

DEFINITION MODULE MathLib;

(* This provides some common mathematical functions. *)

CONST
    pi = 3.141592654; (* This degree of precision *)
    e = 2.718281818; (* might not be provided !   *)

PROCEDURE real(intVal : INTEGER) : REAL;
(* This converts an INTEGER value to a REAL one. *)

PROCEDURE entier(realVal : REAL) : INTEGER;
(* This converts a REAL value to an INTEGER one; *)
(* the nearest-possible INTEGER value is given.   *)

PROCEDURE sqrt(value : REAL) : REAL;
(* This calculates square roots. *)

PROCEDURE exp(value : REAL) : REAL;
(* This calculates exponents of *e*. *)

PROCEDURE ln(value : REAL) : REAL;
(* This calculates logarithms of base *e*. *)

PROCEDURE sin(angle : REAL) : REAL;
(* This calculates the sine of an angle (in radians). *)

PROCEDURE cos(angle : REAL) : REAL;
(* This calculates the cosine of an angle (in radians). *)

```
PROCEDURE arctan(tangent: REAL): REAL;
(* This calculates the angle (in radians) of a tangent. *)
```

```
(* some implementations also provide: *)
```

```
PROCEDURE power(base, power : REAL) : REAL;
(* This calculates general exponents. *)
```

```
PROCEDURE log(value : REAL) : REAL;
(* This calculates logarithms of base ten. *)
```

```
END MathLib.
```

```
DEFINITION MODULE Storage;

(* This provides dynamic memory allocation. *)


    PROCEDURE ALLOCATE(VAR location  : ADDRESS;
                           size      : CARDINAL);
    (* This allocates a memory area from free space *)
    (* of the given size (in storage units); its start   *)
    (* address is returned in the parameter location. *)


    PROCEDURE DEALLOCATE(VAR  location : ADDRESS;
                             size      : CARDINAL);
    (* This frees the memory area with the given   *)
    (* start address and size (in storage units).     *)



(* some implementations also provide: *)


    PROCEDURE Available(size : CARDINAL): BOOLEAN;
    (* This indicates whether the given amount of   *)
    (* memory can be allocated successfully or not. *)


END Storage.
```

DEFINITION MODULE Processes;

(* This provides coroutine scheduling and *)
(* synchronisation by means of *signals*. *)

(* ------ this part is for coroutine creation ------ *)

    PROCEDURE StartProcess(proc   : PROC;
                           wkSpSize : CARDINAL);
    (* This makes a coroutine from the given procedure, *)
    (* then suspends the currently-executing coroutine *)
    (* and starts the new one. Transfers of execution *)
    (* between coroutines are not made by explicit calls *)
    (* of TRANSFER in the coroutines, but implicitly *)
    (* whenever a signal (see below) is sent or awaited. *)
    (* The program ends as soon as any coroutine ends, *)
    (* whether this is the main program module or not. *)

(* ---- this part is for coroutine synchronisation ---- *)

    TYPE
      Signal;   (* signals are variables of this type. *)

    PROCEDURE Init(VAR signal : Signal);
    (* This initialises the given signal variable. *)
    (* Note: This procedure must be called before *)
    (* a signal variable is used for the first time. *)

103

```
PROCEDURE Send(VAR signal : Signal);
(* This emits the given signal. The longest-   *)
(* suspended coroutine awaiting the signal     *)
(* will receive it, and is the one allowed to  *)
(* resume execution. If there is no coroutine  *)
(* currently waiting, the signal is ignored.   *)
(* A transfer of control to another coroutine  *)
(* which is able to execute may still occur.   *)


PROCEDURE Wait(VAR signal : Signal);
(* This suspends the currently-executing coroutine *)
(* until it receives the given signal. The coroutine *)
(* is suspended even if the signal was sent earlier *)
(* and no coroutines were awaiting it at the time.  *)


PROCEDURE Awaited(signal : Signal) : BOOLEAN;
(* This indicates if any coroutines are        *)
(* currently awaiting  the given signal. It *)
(* does not cause any transfer of control.  *)


END Processes.
```

10 Using a Typical Implementation

10.1 General

Implementations can vary in many respects, but their methods of operation are usually quite similar. Each implementation typically consists of two parts, the *compiler* and the *linker*. The compiler translates the original Modula *source-code* held in a *compilation unit* (a file containing an individual program, definition or implementation module) into *object code* (lower-level processor-specific code) which is then saved in an *object-code file*. The linker creates an executable program by merging together a suitable group of object-code files, one belonging to a program module and the others belonging to the various global modules used by the program.

10.2 Compilation

When a module is compiled, the compiler accesses the object-code files of all definition modules imported by the module in order to check that all uses of imported facilities made by the module are consistent with their definitions. The relevant definition modules must therefore have been compiled beforehand. With an implementation module, the equivalent definition module must also have been compiled beforehand.

An implementation module can be recompiled at any time without affecting the compilation of any other module. However, when a definition module is recompiled, **every module which imports it must also be recompiled**. This ensures that all uses of the module remain consistent with the new definition. (The equivalent implementation module must be recompiled as well.) If any of these other modules is also a definition module, further recompilations may be needed. This sometimes leads to a cascade of recompilations being required, and this can take some time to achieve. Recompilation of any definition module in a large system should therefore only be done after careful consideration of the possible consequences!

Some implementations allow compiler options to be embedded in source code, using a special form of comment which begins with a three-character sequence consisting of a dollar symbol, an (upper-case) letter and a condition symbol. No spaces must intervene between the opening comment bracket and this sequence. The letter specifies the option required. The condition symbol specifies its state for subsequent lines of code up to the point where it is changed again: a plus (+) symbol enables the given option, a minus (-) symbol causes it to be disabled, and an equals (=) symbol resets the option to its previous state. Normal comment text can follow an option sequence inside the same comment brackets. Typical comments of this kind are:

```
(*$T-      turn off range-checking here. *)
             . . .
(*$T+      turn it back on again here.   *)
```

Implementation documentation should be consulted for a more detailed description of any options which are available. If this feature is not supported by the compiler, the comment will simply be treated as a normal one, so program portability is not affected in any way by its use.

10.3 Linking

When all modules comprising a program have been compiled, the linker is used to merge the object-code files together into a single executable program. With some implementations, a list of all the required modules must be given; with others, only the program name need be given, and the linker automatically searches for imported modules until the program is complete.

With some implementations, the linker checks that all object-code files are compatible with each other, and signals an error when any necessary recompilations have not been performed. With others, no checking is done, and the user is responsible for ensuring that the program is self-consistent. (A program built from inconsistent object-code files will almost certainly fail to run correctly.)

10.4 File management

A naming standard is often applied to files used with Modula implementations. The file name is usually expected to be the same as the module name, with a suffix added to indicate the type of file. Common suffixes are .**def** for source-code files of definition modules, .**mod** for source-code files of program and implementation modules, .**sym** for object-code files of definition modules, .**obj**, .**rel** or .**lnk** for object-code files of program and implementation modules, and .**prg**, .**exe** or .**lod** for executable programs.

(Problems can sometimes arise from restrictions on the length of file names; a file may appear to be missing because its full name has been truncated by the file system.)

For convenience in managing a system which contains many modules, an implementation based on a reasonably-powerful file system typically allows the user to define a list of file directories. This is used by the compiler to search for object-code files of definition modules, and by the linker to search for all object-code files needed to build a program. If available, such a facility is extremely useful, since it allows most modules to be specified by module name alone, irrespective of where they are located in the file system. Implementation documentation should be consulted for a description of how to set up such a search list, since the method tends to be implementation-specific.

Appendix 1

The ISO/ASCII character set

This is the most commonly-encountered character set used by Modula implementations. For convenience, it is shown below with both decimal and octal numberings. The ordinal number of any character is found by summing the number of the row and column.

Decimal numbering:

	0	1	2	3	4	5	6	7	8	9
0	.nul.	.soh.	.stx.	.etx.	.eot.	.enq.	.ack.	.bel.	.bs.	.ht.
10	.lf.	.vt.	.ff.	.cr.	.so.	.si.	.dle.	.dc1.	.dc2.	.dc3.
20	.dc4.	.nak.	.syn.	.etb.	.can.	.em.	.sub.	.esc.	.fs.	.gs.
30	.rs.	.us.	space	!	"	#	$	%	&	'
40	(	)	*	+	,	-	.	/	0	1
50	2	3	4	5	6	7	8	9	:	;
60	<	=	>	?	@	A	B	C	D	E
70	F	G	H	I	J	K	L	M	N	O
80	P	Q	R	S	T	U	V	W	X	Y
90	Z	[	\	]	^	_	`	a	b	c
100	d	e	f	g	h	i	j	k	l	m
110	n	o	p	q	r	s	t	u	v	w
120	x	y	z	{			}	~	.del.		

Octal numbering:

	0	1	2	3	4	5	6	7
0	.nul.	.soh.	.stx.	.etx.	.eot.	.enq.	.ack.	.bel.
10	.bs.	.ht.	.lf.	.vt.	.ff.	.cr.	.so.	.si.
20	.dle.	.dc1.	.dc2	.dc3.	.dc4.	.nak.	.syn.	.etb.
30	.can.	.em.	.sub.	.esc.	.fs.	.gs.	.rs.	.us.
40	space	!	"	#	$	%	&	'
50	(	)	*	+	,	-	.	/
60	0	1	2	3	4	5	6	7
70	8	9	:	;	<	=	>	?
100	@	A	B	C	D	E	F	G
110	H	I	J	K	L	M	N	O
120	P	Q	R	S	T	U	V	W
130	X	Y	Z	[	\	]	^	_
140	`	a	b	c	d	e	f	g
150	h	i	j	k	l	m	n	o
160	p	q	r	s	t	u	v	w
170	x	y	z	{			}	~	.del.

The first 32 characters and the last character are the (non-printable) control characters.

The ISO international standard allows for variations in some of the characters between national standard versions, so the above tables may differ slightly from the actual set provided by some implementations.

Index

Page numbers in bold face indicate main references.

111

112

113